101 Doggy Dilemmas

Tony Cruse

Publishing Notes

Credits

Words: **Tony Cruse**

Illustrations by **Rebecca M Durbin**

Typesetting by **World Tech**

Acknowledgments

Thank you...

To Andy and Danny, my old bandmates– For the constant badgering during band reunion curry nights! It's your encouragement that kick-started this very book.

To the Association of Pet Dog Trainers (APDT UK) – Thanks for being there for the owners and always considering the welfare of the pet dogs during training.

To the 'Book Panel': Carrie-Anne, Chrisanne, Denise, Lee, Lyn and Malcolm – For helping make some key decisions which lead to this book being the best it can be.

To Dad and Jo – Thanks for the support and fantastic breaks in Spain.

To Denise and all at Clarendon House – For believing in me when my business started up.

To the dogs in my past: Remus, Chips, Lucky, Fizz, Foxy, Merlow – They have all taught me so much and I miss them all.

To my oldest friends in the canine business, Tim and Charlotte. Tim, it's been a long journey ehh? Charlotte, I miss bouncing those ideas around during those leisurely lunchtime walks.

To all the owners and dogs at Galleywoofers Dog Training Club and The Tuesday Club – I can't wish for better customers. Great people and fantastic dogs.

To my assistants at Galleywoofers, past and present: Sarah H, Cheryl, Becky, Amy, Kathy and Caroline – Thanks for keeping me in coffee and being there when it rains!

To Helen Vandenberghe – For guiding this book to completion and for helping to push my career to new heights.

To Motley, my current dog – For the constant source of amusement!

To my Mum, my Sister and her family – Thanks for being my biggest supporters.

To the people who have inspired me in this industry: Jean Donaldson, Ian Dunbar, Patricia McConnell, David Ryan and Sarah Whitehead.

To Sarah and the Your Dog Magazine team – For the opportunity to write on a regular basis and exercise my article ideas in a quality magazine.

To Steve and all at the Institute of Modern Dog Trainers (IMDT) – A great bunch of positive people who train with welfare and knowledge in mind.

To Tracy Jones and Chelmsford Radio – For the laughs during the Sunday Live radio shows. Thanks for the opportunity.

And finally, thanks to my partner, Jo – For the love, support, encouragement, fantastic ideas and decisions (which usually prove correct). xx

- Tony Cruse

Contents...

Introduction

'Your dog should cause you to smile at least once a day'

I hope my line above rings true with you. Our dogs bring us joy, laughter and fun. A good park walk should be a great stress reliever!

But you have to invest in your dog. A little training time goes a long way! Train your dog and enjoy the process.

This book is laid out in a numerical form from number one, all the way through to one-hundred and one. The questions are not laid out in any particular groups - you can dip in and out when you need to. Of course, I'm not stopping you if you want to read it from front cover to back cover in one session!

The one-hundred and one questions are based on the queries I have been asked on phone-in shows, at tea breaks during dog training classes and other places including Pubs. Yes, it appears everyone has a dog with a dilemma! Some questions are a little quirky whilst others are important and can be a matter of concern.

Now you can realise why your dog does odd things, and if those odd things bug you or other people you can now work on a simple solution.

To keep things easy and consistent throughout this book, I have referred to dogs in the male gender. Of course, the dilemmas and solutions apply to all dogs, both female and male. I have also given the various breed names mentioned initial capital letters.

I must stress that if your dog's behaviour suddenly changes, take him to your veterinary surgery for a check-up. Before we address any behavioural issues, we must ensure we have a relatively healthy dog first.

For example, a dog with a dental abscess is likely to be pretty grumpy towards other dogs and people. Medication could solve that dilemma!

If you like training with your dog, consider a reward-based training club. Pop along without your dog, have a look and a chat. If you like what you see, sign up. Dog training should not be a chore! The class should appear fun and rewards should be used, such as toys and food.

Rewards make learning fun and help ensure the task your dog is learning is more likely to be repeated in future.

Finally, there are currently a plethora of methods, equipment and different styles within dog training. Some can hurt the dog and provide negative associations. There is simply no need to physically punish a dog.

We are smarter than that! My style of training is about encouragement and building on success, using rewards. The methods in this book involve teaching the behaviour that we want, which instantly decreases the behaviour, which we don't! For example, a dog rewarded for sitting is a dog who is less likely to jump up.

Enjoy this book and keep it handy. Your dog will thank you for it!

Tony Cruse
Dog Training and Behavioural Issues.
www.tc-dog-training.co.uk

Why does my dog...

Bark at the postman?

The Situation:

Some owners find their dog barks when he sees the uniform, but for others it's when letters come through the letterbox. Some dogs are almost watching the letterbox waiting! It can sound frantic and be quite intimidating to the poor old postie!

Why:

Barking is natural behaviour for dogs. They are generally protective of their environment and being startled by anything can cause barking. Essentially, they are trying to make the intruder go away. Of course, the barking pays off when the postie leaves to continue his round. Is it any surprise that barking continues to be a daily occurrence?

Quick Tips:

The association needs to change from potential 'scary intruder' to 'ooh, it's the postman – I get a reward". Have a word with your postman and let him know you're working on this behaviour with your dog (always good to keep them onside). If your dog tears the mail, then install a letter basket. Put a pot of your dog's favourite treats ready nearby. As soon as your dog sees or hears the postman, grab a few of treats and scatter behind your dog (away from the letter box). For greater control, put your dog on his lead beforehand. It's very important to be consistent – so you could ask a friend to practice this with you (postie outfit optional!) and play the part of the postman.

To advance this, place a chew in the dog's bed as soon as he sees/hears the postman.

What you'll get is a dog that sees the postman, feels good, and goes to his bed.

Why does my dog...

Dig up my garden?

The Situation:

This can be really frustrating when your beloved pet seems intent on ripping up flowerbeds, digging holes and destroying the grass. And it usually occurs just after the bulbs have been planted and your dream of a perfect landscaped garden is ruined in minutes.

Why:

Digging is what canines do in their natural environment – it's a hardwired behaviour from a dog's past. On a hot day a dog will dig a den to provide a cool spot to sleep in. Dogs, such as Terriers, will dig because their genuine working job can be digging out fury animals. As a result, they enjoy digging because it produces endorphins (happy hormones).

Quick Tips:

Hardwired behaviour is very tricky to stop completely, so why not give your dog a 'Fido-friendly' digging area? You can encourage him to dig in this area by hiding his toys in it. You only need about a square metre but you'll need to get him started and dig up a bit of soil. Make it the best digging area for him. If he does start digging up your flowerbed, gently guide him over to his very own digging patch.

You'll find that if he's allowed to dig, he'll often dig less!

Also, ensure your dog is having enough exercise and fun on his regular walks and park trips. He'll dig more when he's bored!

Why does my dog...

Jump up when greeting?

The Situation:

This can be a nightmare – you walk in the door and before you know it you've got paw prints all over you. On a more serious note, a larger dog can knock people completely over, and cause fear in friends and visitors, and especially children.

Why:

Dogs greet other dogs at face level; it's their way of introducing themselves, so they naturally want to do this with us too. Also, jumping up can be a sign of anxiety and the dog seeking approval or reassurance. If the dog could speak he would probably be saying "hello…hello…hello" or "sorry…sorry…sorry". So to physically punish this would be very wrong.

Quick Tips:

Have some of your dog's favourite treats to hand. Before he jumps up drop one on the floor and repeat each time before he attempts to jump. This is teaching that good things happen when 'four paws are on the floor'! However, if he does jump up, turn to the side, quietly look away (no voice, no eye contact), and wait for the four paws on the floor to drop the treat again. You may find that eventually your dog chooses to sit rather than jump…That is worthy of a food reward also! And if he hasn't jumped up for a while, you can go down to his level and fuss him on the floor, if you wish.

For visitors – you can be in control of the treats and drop them to the floor, which will keep his focus downwards. In future, he'll be looking down (for treats) rather than up.

You can regularly rehearse this with a friend. At first you may want to keep your dog on a lead, so your friend can safely move away should your dog jump up.

This has to be consistent with everyone he meets.

Why does my dog...

Run off in the park?

The Situation:

If your dog goes AWOL the instant you unclip his lead, this can cause a lot of stress for you, the owner, and can put both your dog and passers-by in danger. Chasing your dog across the park is not only embarrassing but can actually make things worse.

Why:

Sorry to say, but the park is probably more exciting than you! There are lots of sights, sounds and scents which dogs can't wait to explore. Also, dogs love to play chase – just watch two dogs playing. If you start manically chasing your dog he may just think you're playing his game.

Quick Tips:

If you connect a long line, it can prevent your dog practicing this unwanted action of running away. You have to make yourself as 'valuable' as the environment – so have your dog's favourite toy on you and some yummy treats (things your dog may value).

Walk your dog around the park on a long line occasionally calling him, and moving away from him in an exciting manner.

When he gets to you, whip out his toy or give him a treat. He'll soon see that it's fun and rewarding to come back to his owner when called. Practice this many times during a park walk, releasing him back after once you have rewarded him with a treat or a game.

Once you have this working, then you can take him off the long line, in a quiet environment to begin with. You could use a whistle instead of your voice to call your dog back. He soon learns that the whistle means food or a fun game with you.

Why does my dog...

Chew the wooden table leg? 5

The Situation:

Chair legs, door frames, banisters.... some dogs find these great fun to chew and gnaw at, leaving you worried about splinters and vets bills, and the house in tatters. Some owners even put off ever buying new furniture for fear it will end up in his tummy!

Why:

If you have a puppy it maybe that he is teething and his gums are in pain. It's a way of working through that pain. It may also be a coping strategy for your dog if he is left alone with little else to do. Chewing produces endorphins (happy hormones!), which helps make a dog feel better. Call it stress relief! Similarly, he may have learned he gets attention when he does this. Even a loud reprimand can be seen as rewarding attention to certain dogs.

Quick Tips:

Give your dog something appropriate to chew instead (chew toys, rawhide chews, and for puppies that are teething, try some ice cubes). If you know you are going to be leaving your dog for a while – why not put some of his dinner inside a chew toy such as a Kong. He will spend a while chewing it to produce the food.

Try and prevent your dog from getting to the table and chair legs. Think about which room he stays in. If you do catch your dog chewing furniture – do not reprimand him, but encourage him towards the more appropriate toy or chew. Substitute the table leg for a Nylabone for example.

Why does my dog...
Steal shoes?

The Situation:

Do your shoes end up in the dog basket, covered in slobber and newly 'air conditioned' by your dog? Why is he a shoe collector? This can really frustrate many owners, but is in fact quite simple to fix.

Why:

Sorry to say this, but your shoes and slippers contain a familiar odour and your dog finds this comforting. We all have a unique scent and we only have to touch a clean cloth once for it to be detected by our dogs. So your footwear reeks of you. If he also chews shoes, it can be a coping mechanism to deal with stress such as being left alone or even the fear of being caught stealing!

Similarly, it can be a great game – especially if you start chasing him to obtain the missing shoe.

Quick Tips:

Prevention is always better than cure, so keep your footwear in a safe place, either up high or in a shoebox. If he does get a shoe – rather than chase him, call him to you, and swap it for a tasty treat or favourite toy. At the very least, you'll get a dog that brings your shoes to you! Sometimes, even give the shoe back to him and exchange it again. If you give it back to him, and exchange, it stops becoming a valuable item to steal.

Why does my dog...
Pull on the lead?

The Situation:

Being dragged down the road by your pet dog is no fun, and can be dangerous. Even small dogs can really pull and potentially cause accidents, leaving you feeling like you're being taken for a walk. Does your dog even know you are at the end of the lead? Walking a dog should be a joint activity!

Why:

Dogs naturally walk faster than we do, and want to get from A to B as quickly as possible. Your dog may find something super exciting, such as a lamppost, or another dog, and be desperate to get to it – almost at any cost and without being aware that you are even there. So it can be the pull of an attraction and the fact that your walking pace doesn't quite match your dog's walking pace.

Quick Tips:

Walk your dog before meals and take some of his dinner out with you. You can then feed him, on the move. When the lead is slack, he gets a snack! If the lead goes tight, simply stop with both hands on the end of the lead. Wait it out until the lead goes slack again, continue on, and feed on the go. Keep repeating, until he learns that when he's near you with a slack lead, he gets a treat (this will help you gain focus).

The consequence for pulling is that it will take him longer to get where he wants to go. Therefore, walking with a loose lead gets him a treat and gets him to the park sooner.

Extra tip from Tony:

"Choke Chains are a cruel and outdated piece of equipment – never use any equipment that has a choking or tightening effect. Isn't it better to have a dog that wants to walk next to you, rather than a dog who is forced to by avoiding discomfort?"

Why does my dog...

Beg at the dinner table?

The Situation:

The Situation:
If you've ever experienced a dog that's drooling at your Sunday roast, you'll know how off putting this is. And that needy stare when you are eating?! It can ruin a good meal!

Why:

Your dog may have previously discovered part of a meal on the floor or even been given some from the table. So he has learned that hanging around that area pays off! Dogs repeat what works for them! We expect a dog to exhibit a massive amount of self-control: can you imagine if the tables were turned and you were hungry and he walked in with a tasty steak burger for himself?

Quick Tips:

Firstly, ensure that no person feeds your dog near the table. No sneaky pieces given under the table from little Jimmy!

Instead, use an interactive toy (like a Kong) with some of your dog's meal in it. At your dinnertime, place it either in his bed or a location in the same room as you. He can then enjoy his yummy Kong whilst you're enjoying your meal.

In future, he will be waiting for his Kong at your chosen location, rather than waiting by the dinner table staring at you. As you eat...so will he.

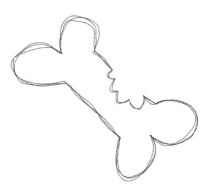

Why does my dog...

Not eat all this food?

The Situation:

If you find half of his food left in his bowl on a regular basis, you might start to worry if something's up. Does he look totally non-plussed as you put the food bowl down?

Why:

If this has suddenly started to occur, check there are no underlying health issues by visiting your vet. However, given the opportunity, some dogs may graze at their food all day. While this isn't necessarily a problem, you're missing a huge opportunity for training and bonding with your dog. If food is constantly around...why rush? Why value it? If something is plentiful, it stops becoming valuable. In the dog's world, food can be a valuable reward and we can harness it within training.

Quick Tips:

Try hand feeding at meal times instead of putting the food in a bowl. You can incorporate some basic training during the meal session. He will associate being with you with a good thing (getting fed), which will increase the training bond.

Using the food as a reward, you can also practice training exercises such as loose-lead walking, recall and sit. In this way, the food becomes more valuable as a result.

If you do feed him in his food bowl and he hasn't eaten it within ten minutes, remove the bowl and present it at the next mealtime.

Why does my dog...
Chase cars?

The Situation:

If your pet loves to chase moving cars, you might find yourself being pulled into the traffic when on lead, and worried about ever letting your dog off lead. The situation could be a real traffic hazard and make walking your dog very difficult.

Why:

Many dogs have a chase instinct whilst other dogs have a herding instinct. Something that moves can provoke this 'hardwired' behaviour, a bit like a reflex. It's a mixed-up instinctual behaviour, instead of herding sheep for example, the Collie could chase cars, circle them and even nip at the tyres. Instead of chasing the rabbit, the Lurcher may feel the need to chase the car.

Quick Tips:

Keep your dog on a lead, so he can't rehearse this behaviour.

If your dog starts to pull, stand very still and remain quiet. If you say anything, this is giving attention to the behaviour you don't want. Your voice can be seen as rewarding, leading to further unwanted behaviour. Keep your feet shoulder-width apart so he will not throw you off-balance. Consider a body harness for your dog. A harness will provide support and protect your dog's neck whilst you are training.

Whilst ignoring it can help extinguish the unwanted behaviour, you could also give your dog a tasty treat a second before he starts to chase. So cars going past mean a tasty treat from you and not something to chase.

Why does my dog...

Chase Joggers?

The Situation:

You're enjoying a nice walk, and all is going well until some joggers pass by and suddenly your placid pet wants to join in the fun, and is off and chasing them down the path.

Why:

Most dogs are born with an instinctive behaviour to chase. If something moving (like a jogger) goes past, they are off without a second thought because that instinct is triggered. There is usually no final aim and when the dog catches up with the jogger often nothing else occurs. This chase could be linked to a primitive predatory pattern, where chase was a big factor and has never been completely bred out of a dog.

Quick Tips:

You have about a five second window of opportunity to break the pattern of, 'dog sees.... dog chases'!

As he spots the jogger, excitedly say your dog's name and give him a treat by tossing it onto the ground. Or even better, excitedly say your dog's name to gain his attention and gently toss a toy or a tennis ball in the other direction to the jogger. Both methods interrupt the chase pattern and redirect it. Instinctual behaviour is very hard to alleviate but over time your dog will see a jogger and look to you for a treat or a chance to CHASE a treat, a toy or a tennis ball! You are then redirecting an instinctual behaviour towards something far more appropriate!

Why does my dog...
Nip my children?

The Situation:

This is particularly common with puppies. Lots of kids love playing with puppies but don't really understand how puppies think.

No surprise, children can be shocked and upset if they are nipped. This can lead to a long-term fear of dogs, and is even more worrying if it's someone else's kids.

Why:

This conduct is common, quite natural but not appropriate. A young dog explores the world using his mouth. During the height of excitement, the line between the toy and the child playing often blurs – sometimes this is accidental, and sometimes the puppy has learned it gets a reaction and attention. Any attention (such as a reprimand) can be seen as rewarding to a puppy. Therefore, he is more likely to repeat it. As far as the puppy is concerned it may even add to the game.

Quick Tips:

As soon as teeth make contact with skin – whether accidental or to get a reaction – then end the game immediately. Remove the toy for at least one minute. Then decide if you want to resume the game or to separate the child and the puppy if he is still overexcited.

Never reprimand the puppy or physically chastise him. He doesn't know; he hasn't learned right from wrong yet. Your job is to teach him.

Alternatively, if the puppy nips the child when there is no toy present, you can re-direct the puppy away from the child and on to a toy. The puppy needs to learn that nipping toys is the best and more fun choice.

For safer management you could have your puppy wear a house line (a long light lead) during playtime. If you are at all concerned, you can guide your puppy away easily.

Why does my dog...

Pee in the house?

The Situation:

When you've done a great job house training during the puppy stage, it can be a bit of a shock when your dog starts to urinate in the house again. Not only is there the hygiene issue to consider, if this is a dramatic change in behaviour it could signal other issues.

Why:

Firstly ensure there are no underlying health issues. Your vet can investigate this further.

One accident can occur because you've forgotten to let the dog out, or maybe your dog is just getting lazy – and so the pattern can develop. And it is worth knowing that the lingering scent of the previous urine can then trigger a reoccurrence.

Quick Tips:

Return to puppy basics. Allow your dog out every two hours and reward him with yummy food straight after he urinates. Be there when he gets it right so you can reward him.

Never punish a dog for urinating in the house. He will simply start avoiding you and probably do it anyway!

Clean up with specialised dog urine cleaner to kill the scent. Be sure to avoid any ammonia-based cleaners; to a dog, stale urine smells very similar to ammonia!

Why does my dog...

Howl when I'm not there?

The Situation:

Many owners are blissfully unaware that their dogs are howling while they're out of the house. That is, until the neighbours start complaining! Not only can this make you the 'bad neighbour', it can signify that your dog may be in distress. Definitely one to get sorted for everyone's sake!

Why:

It is believed that the howl is produced specifically to call members of the family back home. This indicates that the dog is feeling lonely and perhaps anxious, so we need to address the cause and then the symptom (the howling) should disappear.

Quick Tips:

Give your dog something to amuse himself with as you leave the house, such as a 'Kong' containing yummy treats or his meal. A Kong is a hollow rubber toy allowing you to stuff it with food.

Another option is to 'Scatter Feed' – e.g. leave a trail of your dog's dry food around the house before you leave. He will spend a grand old time hunting for the pieces and even when finished, he will still be sniffing for more. Keep the radio on for some background noise.

Build up the duration of your absence in small stages, so that your dog gradually gets used to you returning. Go out of the front door for thirty seconds and re-enter. Then increase to sixty seconds. Each time returning before he starts to howl and get anxious.

Ensure your dog has had enough exercise and stimulation before you leave.

Why does my dog...
Roll in fox scent?

The Situation:

You've just given your perfect pet a lovely wash and you're out on his walk but before you know it he's wriggling on his back in the grass. No, this isn't just a cute attempt to get tummy tickles! He's probably rolling in fox scent! There is no mistaking the odour of fox poop!

Why:

There are many theories about this. Perhaps to a dog, fox-scent smells so good! It's like his very own aftershave. Some believe the fox scent is used to disguise his odour when he is hunting food. Perhaps an old behaviour remaining from those primitive dog days.

You may notice your dog does this more after he's been washed, Maybe he prefers a natural scent to your lovely synthetic shampoo? He certainly smells more 'animal' after rolling in it!

Quick Tips:

If it frequently occurs, keep your dog on a lead or a long line. Whilst on the walk look for the tell-tale signals in his body language, such as lots of interested sniffing and crouching down.

Try and interrupt him before he hits the deck with a recall or guide him away if using the long line. Alternatively use the 'leave' request. To a dog, a good 'leave' command means you are going to present him with something tasty. He soon learns to look away from the thing you are telling him to leave.

Why does my dog...

Chase cats?

The Situation:

Many dogs love to chase cats and other small animals. While this can seem amusing at first, like something out of 'Tom & Jerry', you'll soon find yourself unpopular with the local cat-owning community! On a more serious note, your dog may be so focused on the cat that he runs into a road or towards another dangerous situation.

Why:

The dog was naturally a predator. He has an inbuilt pattern, which is see/stalk/chase/bite/kill/eat. Many domestic dogs, although not all, have the first three of that scale. The other parts have generally been bred out. Chasing is strong hardwired behaviour and the dog feels self-rewarded when exhibiting it. Chasing is an instinctual behaviour in many dogs.

Quick Tips:

Don't allow your dog to strengthen this behaviour by practicing it. Keep him on a long-line or lead. The split second he sees the animal, say his name and pop a piece of yummy chicken into his mouth. After a time, the cat or small animal can become the tip-off that snacks will appear from you!

When walking him, try and keep your distance from any creature he may chase. The closer he is the more intense his reaction. Also, if you spook a cat into running, it provokes the chase instinct I mentioned earlier. Try and walk safely by at a good distance. Perhaps tell your dog, 'Hey it's only a pussycat. No big deal!'

Why does my dog...

Sniff other dogs?

The Situation:

You're walking along in the park and another dog approaches. Before you know it your pet dog has ground to a sudden halt and seems intent on sniffing the rear end of his new friend. You and the other owner look away and discuss the weather.

Why:

Dogs view the world 'through their noses'! Their noses contain over one-hundred-and-fifty million sensory receptors, which tells them all they need to know about the other dog. The sex, the age, the health and breeding ability are all pieces of information gained by a good sniff! Dogs tend to nose target the areas where pheromones ('social odours') are released such as the ears, muzzle, paws and particularly the back end. Simply, it is part of a dog's social greeting.

Quick Tips:

Whilst you can allow your dog to greet some dogs when out on a walk, you don't have to allow him to greet all other dogs. On many occasions simply keep walking. If you want them to greet, try and keep your lead loose and allow the dogs to sniff each other.

If your dog is denied a meeting too often or if the lead is tight, frustration can build leading to barking and lunging.

Why does my dog...
Lick me all the time?

The Situation:

You walk in the door and before you know it you've had a complete facial wash thanks to your dog! Hands, knees, feet – they're all fair game in the licking competition that dogs seem to have invented. Although this can be endearing, are you sure you know what your dog has just had in his mouth before he licks you?

Why:

Our soft skin has a salty taste that our dogs may like. It also usually gets a reaction which maybe as subtle as a laugh. This reaction encourages the licking next time. And so the dog's routine greeting becomes a happy licking-fest.

It is also thought that licking is a pacifying action, often seen when puppies lick their mothers' mouths.

Quick Tips:

It is very simple to stop this licking. The second your dog licks, end the greeting. Stand up, cut off any eye contact and avoid any physical contact for thirty seconds. It may take many repetitions but over time your dog learns that licking doesn't pay off. The party ends! If it becomes difficult, simply walk into another room and shut the door for thirty seconds.

An alternative would be to give your dog something else to do, like carry a toy in his mouth instead. He can't do both! So at times when he would normally lick you, pull out the toy and allow him to hold it in his mouth instead.

Why does my dog...
Cower from people trying
to pet him?

The Situation:

Out on a walk and a well intending neighbour reaches to pet your dog. He cowers and moves away as if he's threatened? Do you beat him at home? He should like all people shouldn't he?

Why:

The size difference between a human and a dog is relatively big. Consider being the size of your dog and looking up at a hand shooting out to you. It can be intimidating for your dog. Also, it can be dependent on how much he was handled as a puppy during the socialisation period and whether being fussed and petted was a pleasant experience. We assume puppies and dogs like physical fuss but not all animals do.

There is a small chance he was physically punished but it is often that he simply doesn't like strangers' hands coming towards him!

Quick Tips:

When you get your puppy, spend his mealtimes hand feeding each piece of his meal to him. Straight away, he sees hands as good things. Hands provide, they don't take away and they don't hurt.

If your dog is hand shy...respect that. Not all humans are tactile either. Allow people to gain your dog's trust by letting your dog approach the person rather than the person approaching your dog.

Why does my dog...

Eat poop?

20

The Situation:

The shame! You turn your head for a moment and when you look back your sweet dog seems to be making a three course meal out of another animal's poop or even his own! Suddenly being licked by your dog is far less appealing.. and what about the bugs he might pick up?

Why:

Coprophagia is the act of eating poop. One of the reasons it is thought that dogs eat poop is to try and make up for a lack of nutrients which may be missing from their current diet. They may have also learned by watching their mother, who would have cleaned out the whelping area by eating the puppies' waste. Either way, the poop eating behaviour is often increased by our reaction, which includes chasing the dog and making a scene - all of which can be rewarding to the dog. He may even consider it a game.

Quick Tips:

Ensure your dog is on a suitable diet. You can speak to your vet about this.

Prevent and manage roaming and eating by keeping your dog on a lead or a long line.

Never punish or startle your dog for this. A smart dog will start to avoid you, run off and do it anyway!

The second he shows any interest in the poop, call his name and toss some yummy treats in the other direction. As he sniffs and eats the treats, you have time to pick up the mess to prevent him from eating it.

For a particularly tricky serial offender, consider muzzling your dog as this prevents the behaviour from occurring and can often break the habit.

Why does my dog...

Know when I am about

to leave the house?

The Situation:

You are just off out and before you have even put on your shoes, your dog is in front of you looking slightly anxious. Is he psychic? Has he a sixth sense? How does he know you're leaving him for the evening?

Why:

Dogs spend most of their waking day watching you and forming associations. For example, 'If my owner has a cup in her hand, she is about to sit down'. Your dog detects little triggers such as picking up your keys, putting on your shoes, picking up your coat. These are all tip-offs that you are going leave him. And we can't rule out scent. Going out for the night wearing aftershave or perfume? These are smelly triggers and a big tip-off that you are leaving.

Similarly, we have set routines because society demands them! We are creatures of habit. Your dog picks up on these routines simply by watching you.

Quick Tips:

Think about giving your dog something pleasant to do when you leave him. The very last thing you can do before opening the front door to exit, can be grabbing a Kong toy stuffed with his dinner or treats. So rather than your dog being anxious about you leaving, you picking up your car keys or jacket become the predictors of a yummy Kong to chew and lick when he is left alone.

You can desensitise him to certain triggers like car keys and jackets by randomly picking them up throughout the day and putting them down again. Bluff! Occasionally put your jacket on and remove it. Those items soon stop being the predictors of you leaving him. But be aware of patterns, for example, shoes...jacket...keys, in that order, means you are leaving him.

Why does my dog...

shake his body?

The Situation:

Sometimes you might notice your pet shaking his body in an unusual way. Almost like a whole body, head to tail shake. It's like he's trying to shake something off.

Why:

It is thought that the body shake or 'shake-off' is a way of resetting after a social situation. You can sometimes spot it after stroking your dog or after two dogs have met. They generally 'shake-off' at the end of the greeting before they carry on their way.

It is possibly a fixed primitive behaviour, where the animal is shaking off the scent of another. As well as loosening up the muscles after the slight tension that a greeting can bring.

Quick Tips:

During a dog to dog social greeting, it is often hard to know when to separate them and carry on your walk. Wait for the shake-off! Then say your dog's name and off you go. Your dog almost indicates by a 'shake-off' that the greeting is over.

Watch when two dogs greet and often you get a synchronised 'shake off'. It is something special to see!

Why does my dog...

Get growly and look

aggressive when suddenly woken up?

The Situation:

You walk past your dog, and one minute he's sound asleep, but step slightly in the wrong direction, and you might find him up on his paws growling at you like you're an intruder.

Why:

For many animals, it is natural to react in a defensive way when startled. They do not know that the intention may be a good one or a mistake. If your dog is of a nervous disposition, then you will likely have seen this already. There are often a few seconds before he realises who you are and that you are not a threat.

Quick Tips:

The old adage, 'Let sleeping dogs lie' is a good one. Keep children away from a dog's usual sleeping environment to avoid accidentally startling the dog. If you have to wake your dog, do it gently by using his name.

Startling a nervous dog can lead to a bite. Always be careful around a sleeping dog. It is no joke and can be particularly unpleasant to be suddenly awoken.

Allow your dog a 'safe haven', where he can sleep in peace knowing he will not be bothered by children or other dogs. It can be incredibly stressful for any animal if they cannot gain adequate restful sleep.

Why does my dog...
Bark at other dogs?

The Situation:

Some dogs bark at every dog that passes them by, whilst others seem to ignore some but need to bark at others. You may even see a pattern in the type or size of the dogs that your dog barks at. But why?

Why:

A dog barks for a variety of different reasons and each has a different tone and pattern. If your dog is indoors, behind a gate or fence then the bark is likely to be one of frustration. A dog's natural conduct is to discover as much about the other dog as possible. The barrier prevents this and so a frustration bark begins, which can sound quite aggressive.

If barking at other dogs occurs outdoors and on walks it maybe also a frustration issue because the dog is on-lead.

However, barking also occurs as communication to the other dog to stay away. It could be that he has had a negative experience around that type of dog in the past or as a puppy was never exposed to that breed.

Quick Tips:

Try and block the gaps in a fence so the dog cannot see the other dogs pass by. Close the curtains so the other dogs cannot be seen from indoors.

Never reprimand your dog for barking because the whole situation starts becoming full of tension. As well as being scared of the other dog, he will anticipate you being angry!

A tight lead probably predicts tension so try and keep the lead loose. Speak happily to your dog as he sees another dog, but before he barks. Perhaps give him a treat before he barks. He will start to see other dogs as the predictor of good stuff!

Why does my dog...

Jump on the sofa?

The Situation:

You're just settling down for an evening's telly, and before you know it, your dog has joined you on the sofa. Alternatively you may find that he only does this when you're out of sight, but the evidence of paw prints, or a warm dog-shaped dent remains!

Why:

Purely and simply, the dog likes the sofa because it is comfy!! If you encourage him on the sofa when you are watching television then he may well sleep on there when you are not watching television. He does not understand there are set times!

Aside from being a snug place to lie, it is off the ground and in an area where he can survey the environment for any changes, such as people coming and going.

Quick Tips:

If you don't mind your dog on the sofa some of the time you can make a rule such as 'when this blanket/towel/mat is on the couch, you are allowed to sleep on it'. After a while the visual cue (of the mat, for example) is learned. If he gets on the sofa without the visual cue, stand up and gently guide him off.

If you never want him on the sofa, shut the living room door during the day to prevent the unwanted behaviour from becoming a habit. Ensure no member of the family is allowing him up. If he jumps up, very quietly guide him off. Place his bed or mat on the floor and make that the best place for him to be. You can give him a treat when he is on the mat or in his bed so that becomes the place he gets fuss and attention.

Why does my dog...

Play tuggy?

The Situation:

You're about to hand your dog his favourite toy but instead of just taking it and playing with it – he seems intent in wrestling it from you. When he actually gets the toy, it's not as much fun anymore. It's as though he enjoys the tugging more than receiving the toy to play with. What's all that about then?

Why:

It is thought that dogs have enjoyed this because it was part of their primitive eating ritual. Two dogs would work at tearing the carcass in this way. These days, many dogs enjoy the game with a tug-toy such as a rope toy. It's not about who wins so much as the engagement. Old-fashioned advice suggested that 'tuggy' could make your dog aggressive but research has since found that this is not the case.

A game of tuggy makes for a superb reward, after a recall, for example. It's also a good way to bond with your dog.

Quick Tips:

Before you play tuggy with your dog, it is a good idea to teach a release command like 'drop'. The reward for releasing the tug-toy is a chance to re-engage and play again! The dog starts to oblige because he trusts that the tug-toy will not be immediately removed.

End the game if your dog accidentally puts his teeth on your hand or arm. This teaches him to play more carefully.

It's not a good idea to play tuggy with a puppy who is teething, as it can be painful enough to put him off the game forever, which would be a real shame.

Why does my dog...

Bark at strangers?

The Situation:

Your placid pet is a joy to be around at home and with people he knows, but when someone new appears he may suddenly turn into his evil twin and start barking like crazy. For new owners, this can really take them by surprise.

Why:

Dogs spend a certain amount of time learning who to trust. A dog learns to relax around familiar people. However, should a new person enter that environment, the dynamics change. Also, some dogs, such as the German Shepherd Dog, have been bred to have a strong guarding instinct and may bark at anyone unfamiliar.

Quick Tips:

Whenever a new person enters the house, you can give your dog a high-value treat, such as a piece of chicken. Eventually, the visitor can give the dog a treat too. Over time, your dog will realise that visitors mean yummy snacks from you and not a scary intruder.

Never allow unfamiliar visitors to approach your dog. This can appear threatening. Allow your dog to approach them when he is happy and ready.

Don't reprimand your dog for barking as it can appear like you are joining in with the tense behaviour.

Put him in another room and only release him when he is quiet. He will soon realise that by not barking, he gets the introduction, which also will be a positive one as it involves treats.

Why does my dog...
Not like the vets?

The Situation:

When Fido is ill, you need to get him to the vets fast. But many owners find the whole experience extremely stressful, not to mention how their dogs feel! Dogs show they are not happy with a situation in a whole range of ways, which may include signs of aggression, barking, shaking etc. Not the best start for a health visit.

Why:

Often a puppy's first trip to a vet surgery is to receive an injection. This can be a traumatic first experience and first experiences stick! Being prodded and poked by a stranger and then having an injection can be an ordeal. Even adult dogs can make a negative association. The next time the dog goes into the surgery, the sights, sounds and smells trigger a memory of the last uncomfortable time and so the dog either wants out by escaping, freezing or maybe by showing signs of aggression. For a dog, aggression can be used to move the 'scary' vet away.

Quick Tips:

Visit your vet surgery frequently without an appointment. Enter the waiting room, weigh your dog, give your dog a yummy treat and leave! Maybe go straight to the park or somewhere your dog enjoys. After a while, a trip to the vets does not predict an examination or injection because it's frequently a short and rewarding experience.

If you have a puppy, consider joining a puppy party at your veterinary surgery. These puppy parties are informative and, if held correctly, can provide your puppy with bags of fun and positive experiences. So from the very beginning, the vet surgery is seen as a great place to visit!

Why does my dog...

Get sick in the car?

The Situation:

You're off for a walk further afield, or maybe you're taking your puppy away for a few days, but your journey is quickly interrupted with the worrying sounds of your dog being sick. Having experienced this once, many owners avoid taking their dogs on longer journeys – but that doesn't have to be the case.

Why:

This is very common with puppies. It often occurs during the drive from the breeder, which is a traumatic event and is coupled with the motion of the car. This could cause vomiting or messing, so from day one your dog believes the car is not a good place to be.

Quick Tips:

Should your puppy be sick, try not to fuss or make it a traumatic event. Be cool, pull over and clean it up.

The good news is you can change the association of a car journey from a bad one to a good one and most dogs will stop being sick on journeys. The key is to make each early journey very short so that the dog has no time to feel sick.

And if the journey ends at a pleasant and rewarding location, it starts being the predictor of something good! Several short journeys to the park or even around the block and arriving back at home for his dinner can help. You can then slowly build up the duration of the journey making the destination fun. You may get the odd blip but keep working at it, so your dog feels better and grows up to become an adult dog who is not frequently sick.

Why does my dog...

Ignore me?

The Situation:

When we get a dog, we often assume it will be a world filled with 'Lassie' moments, when he will constantly be running into our arms, and be our most loyal companion. It can be a bit of a shock then when you get the cold shoulder, and your pet ignores your commands, and doesn't want your attention.

Why:

Unfortunately, human nature is to often pay attention when the dog is doing something mischievous. We use his name, shout and frequently say 'no'. The words are often said harshly and usually end with the dog being denied the fun he was having. So is it any wonder when he hears our voice and ignores it? Unfortunately it is not like Disney and your dog will not comply because 'he should' or because 'he wants to please'.

Quick Tips:

We can hand feed our dogs at meal times and engage with fun games such as fetch and tuggy. Taking your dog to a reward-based training club can also increase that bond. We need to be seen as providers.

Try and reward your dog more for the behaviour you like rather than shout 'no' at the behaviour you don't. Teach name recognition, say his name and follow it with a treat or a piece of his meal. The more you do this, the more you build a reflex. Responding to you often pays off for Fido... so he starts doing it more!

Why does my dog...

Follow me everywhere?

The Situation:

Do you have a stalker? As you move from room to room in the house, do you find you have your own personal 'shadow' going everywhere you go? Whilst this can seem very cute and gratifying at first, you may start to wonder if this is normal.

Why:

Dogs are social animals and like nothing better than spending time with us. They often spend the first six weeks of life in their new home with us and then suddenly everyone disappears to work and school. The contrast is massive! This can leave a dog unable to cope.

The next time your dog sees you he is unlikely to let you out of his sight for fear that you will leave him again. This results in him following you from room to room. A dog that follows to that extent is usually not a confident dog.

It can lead to a lonely dog who copes by chewing and destroying the house.

Quick Tips:

Getting a second dog may not help the situation. It is a gamble and you could end up with two anxious dogs! It's far better to teach your dog how to cope alone.

If he follows you everywhere, you can start by gently shutting the door behind you to prevent him from following you. In the early stages, you only need close it for ten seconds. You build this time up slowly; each time the door is shut for longer ensuring he does not get the time to become worried.

If you are leaving the house without him, give him a tasty pre-filled Kong to enjoy whilst you are gone. He should start looking forward to you leaving because he gets the yummy Kong. Licking and chewing also has a calming effect that can help when he is alone.

Why does my dog...

Bark at strange objects?

The Situation:

Is it a bird? Is it a plane? Is it a plastic bag blowing in the wind? It could be any 'everyday' item that triggers a reaction in your dog. If your dog freaks out at strange and unusual objects, this can really catch you off guard, and turn a normal walk into a minefield.

Why:

During the first sixteen weeks of a dog's life, they are like sponges, seeing things for the first time whilst remaining relatively fearless and adapting best to the situation. If during this 'socialisation period', the dog had not seen a wheelchair, for example, when he is older he may not be able to compute that it is not a threat. Barking at the wheelchair is the result. Barking is often the result of fear and a way to gain space between him and the 'scary' thing!

Also, it is thought that dogs go through a 'fear period'. This is perfectly normal and is a time in their development where they are more wary of objects, sometimes familiar objects. Understand this and try not to make it traumatic by remaining relatively cool and calm.

Quick Tips:

During the first sixteen weeks, safely expose your puppy to as many objects and people as possible. Make each experience a good one, so the use of treats can help. For example, 'umbrella up...treat appears'.

Never drag your dog towards anything he is scared of. Although your dog may be barking and lunging, chances are he is fearful. Don't make a big scene. Coolly guide him away to a distance where he can cope. Often increasing the distance decreases the fear.

Give your dog time to 'compute' and absorb the strange object. Perhaps talk nicely to him as he is looking at it, 'Hey, it's only a wheelie bin. No problem'.

Why does my dog...
Steal food?

The Situation:

Watch out, watch out, there's a thief about! Have you found snacks going missing when you turn your back? Or maybe your pet is more brazen and grabs food right off the table or plate. Apart from being frustrating when your pet has gobbled your dinner, if allowed to persist this could become a safety issue, especially if you have toddlers who wander around with food in their hands.

Why:

Simply, dogs are naturally 'opportunistic scavengers'. It is part of their build.

Dogs have survived to become an extremely successful species by eating what they stumble upon at any time of day or night. Without any learning, this is what a dog will do in the home.

Food isn't stolen out of spite or to become 'pack leader' but because the food is available and accessible. Perhaps it's the actions of an intelligent dog?

Quick Tips:

Build a good domestic routine where your dog always eats at roughly the same time of day. If food is expected, it can stop it being of such a high value, so it is not frequently stolen.

Stop any habits forming by not leaving food in accessible places, for example leaving a bacon sandwich on a coffee table will be too much for most dogs! And for some peckish humans too!! Prevention is the main solution; keep work surfaces free of food.

Teach a good 'leave' command, which you can use in an emergency or use a reliable recall to call your dog away from the food and towards you.

Why does my dog...
Chew his tail?

34

The Situation:

You'd think your pet had enough things to chew, with all the toys he's got but, no, he seems to be insistent on creating his own 'chew toy' with his tail.

Why:

This can be a coping strategy, for example, if the dog is anxious about being left alone. Chewing produces endorphins and can help to calm. The dog may be looking for something to chew and settles for his tail. It can then become infected and irritating, which then makes it even more interesting to investigate and chew. It can become a vicious circle which is hard to interrupt. Tail chewing can also be a sign of a health issue. If a dog cannot investigate the sore area, the closest he may be able to reach is his tail. For example, it is common for a dog with irritating anal glands to chew the base of his tail.

Quick Tips:

To find out if your dog is telling you something, visit your vet who will check the anal glands and your dog's general health.

Ensure he has enough exercise and stimulation (greetings, exercise, sniffing, playing etc) in his daily life.

Try and find the cause but you can break the habit with the use of an Elizabethan Collar (head cone) or a muzzle so that your dog can't access his tail.

Leave your dog plenty of chew toys and perhaps a Kong with his dinner in it. He will chew the Kong to get the food out.

Why does my dog...
Sleep on my bed?

The Situation:

You're just settling down for a good night's sleep and before you know it you hear heavy breathing, and whiff that distinctive doggy odour. Yes, Rover's come to bed. Or maybe, it's when you're out of the house, and when you return you discover 'someone's been sleeping in your bed'!

Why:

We all agree our beds are comfortable and it seems your dog has worked it out too! It's snug and off the floor, meaning your dog feels snug and safe up there.

Your bed also contains your scent, which is familiar and comforting for your pet. This can be despite having clean sheets. Dogs have such a powerful nose that it can take several washes to completely remove the odour from material.

Quick Tips:

Many people happily allow their dogs to share their bed. It is a choice. However, if it is a problem for you then prevention is the key. 'Shut the bedroom door' is the simplest solution! If a dog is unable to practice the unwanted behaviour, he will not perform it and the habit dies.

If you do want to allow your dog to sleep on your bed, it is wise to teach an 'off' command first. Invite him up, show him a treat and toss it onto the bedroom floor whilst saying, 'off'. After twenty or so repetitions he will leave the bed when you say, 'off' and bluff the throw.

Why does my dog...
Bark at the window?

The Situation:

You might be enjoying a night in front of the TV but Rover seems to get his entertainment from barking at anything that passes the window. People walking past, dustcarts, anything that moves or makes a noise can set your pet off causing a stressful household.

Why:

Most dogs have been bred to alert us if there is an intruder. People walking past your window could be seen as a threat. Your dog barks and the people keep walking, so he may believe his barking is working and is removing the perceived threat. The behaviour of barking is then repeated next time, often getting louder and more intense.

Alert breeds, such as terriers, tend to bark at anything that moves or makes a noise, so having a window on a busy street can be a problem.

Quick Tips:

Net curtains or blinds can help blur the moving objects and shutting the curtain blanks them out completely. Having the radio on in the background makes any street noises less noticeable.

Don't shout at your dog or reprimand him if he is barking as it may sound like you are joining in and perhaps there really is a threat to be concerned about.

Some dogs can get used to activity outside of the window once they learn there is no threat and that their owners don't jump up and down and shout.

However, if he continues to react, call his name and place a piece of his dinner in another room the second he sees something he may bark at. If repeated, he will learn that people walking past are not a threat and they predict snacks!

Why does my dog...

Get excited when I get

the lead out?

37

The Situation:

Getting out for a simple walk can be a challenge and really quite stressful if every time you pick up the lead your dog goes into hyperdrive. Whether it's jumping, barking, running onto the furniture – this over-excitement can get your walk off on the wrong paw.

Why:

Over the weeks and months, the lead appears, gets clipped on and an exciting walk occurs. In that order. Due to something called Classical Conditioning the lead soon becomes the predictor of the fun walk. Whether the walk occurs or not, your dog gets excited by the sight and sound of his lead.

Quick Tips:

You can start again and make the lead the predictor of nothing special. This is done by visiting the place where you keep his lead, taking hold of it and walking around the house for ten seconds before placing back. Do this randomly throughout the day, perhaps fifteen times. Initially, he will become excited but soon learns that every time the lead is picked up a walk does not always follow. Over time, this method will make the situation less chaotic for you and your dog when you do take him for a walk.

You can apply the above method to any article that excites your dog. Randomly pick up the door keys and put them down again, put your jacket on and remove it. You are breaking the tight association created by these triggers.

Why does my dog...

Get excited when I

arrive home?

38

The Situation:

It's lovely to be wanted but if anyone else jumped on you, licked your face or barked as you came through the door, you'd have something to say about it! Allowing your dog to do this can upset family and guests and probably doesn't set the best tone when you get through the door.

Why:

Dogs are social creatures and when a familiar person arrives home, they are more than pleased. Often his excitement spills over into chaos. The more we fuss the dog and mirror his excitement, the more excited he gets next time you arrive home.

Quick Tips:

Always remember, 'Calm exits and cool entrances'. You then leave your dog, so he is not excited and when entering you do not reinforce any chaos. When you return, acknowledge your dog but keep it cool. After ten minutes or so and when he is calmer you can give him the fuss that you know he deserves.

Or perhaps you can redirect this excitement towards a toy. Call it a 'hello toy'. As you enter the house, say hello to your dog and then produce this toy. For some dogs such as Golden Retrievers, carrying a toy in their mouth can pacify excited behaviour.

For visitors, you can request that your dog sits. And only when sitting can he receive the attention he wants. He will learn a 'sit' means a good greeting. This can be useful because it keeps him in one place and he can't be jumping up whilst he is sitting!

Why does my dog...
Bark at the doorbell?

The Situation:

Do you have your own personal warning system? If every time your doorbell rings, your dog reacts by barking, this can be really off-putting to your visitors – not to mention the postie and delivery people. It's also more likely to stress you out, meaning you might not be your usual cool, calm self.

Why:

Dogs soon learn that the sound of the doorbell predicts somebody behind the door. This can make a dog anxious or excited. Due to 'Classical Conditioning', pretty soon the bell alone can evoke crazy barking...no visitors required!

It is very common and to stop a dog barking completely is extremely difficult. For centuries, humans have bred dogs to bark! But rather than having frequent and noisy barking, you could aim for one bark only. An alert bark can be useful.

Quick Tips:

If possible change the ringtone of your doorbell. Ring it and whilst showing the dog a treat, lure him into his bed where he gets the treat. Repeat many, many times by carefully setting up the situation (relative rings bell when you are ready). Over time, that particular chime will mean a snack in your dog's bed and he will make his way there rather than barking at the front door. If you are out or you are not around to treat your dog in his bed, protect your brand new chime and the association it brings by switching back to the old one or turning it off.

If your doorbell comes with two push-buttons, put one on the door as usual and have one in your pocket. Randomly walk near your dog and press it. Follow it by tossing a treat into your dog's bed. Again you are building that association...bell = treat in bed.

Never reprimand your dog for barking, it sounds like you are joining in! Acknowledge your dog once and then walk away.

Why does my dog...
Cower at thunder and
lightning?

The Situation:

It's never nice to see your dog distressed. When there is thunder and lightning outside, some will try to bury themselves under the furniture, or shake uncontrollably and drool. This just shows you how stressed they are when this happens.

Why:

Some dogs are genetically more noise sensitive than others. And as an owner, you often behave slightly differently when a storm occurs and your dog can pick up on that. The anxious behaviour can also happen during fireworks. It is natural behaviour for any animal to be apprehensive of something it cannot understand.

Quick Tips:

During a storm, never ignore your dog but do not change your behaviour too much. Be cool and speak happily to him.

Always give him a 'safe haven' to escape to, should he so wish. A 'safe haven' can be a snug dog bed under a table or an open crate with a blanket over it. Allow him to be alone if he chooses. Turn on a radio as background noise.

If you know a storm is approaching, create a yummy Kong. Stuff some tasty food inside and keep it until you hear the first crash of thunder. Place it in his bed or 'safe haven' and let him enjoy it. He will feel good as the storm travels over. Your dog may soon realise thunder is not a threat and after a while the thunder actually predicts good things such as a stuffed Kong.

Why does my dog...

Not do as I say?

41

The Situation:

You say his name, once twice, three times. No response. It takes four commands to get him to sit. Sometimes only shouting works. Is your dog deaf? Is he ignoring you?

Why:

Dogs are animals and in the animal world nothing is done without reason or some benefit. Whether it is freezing on one spot to avoid confrontation or sitting waiting for food to arrive...both are done for a reason. Dogs will not do things because 'they should' or because 'they respect you'. In modern dog training, we try and use the potential of gaining something pleasant as a motivator. A dog sits pretty fast once he learns that if he sits he may get a piece of his meal, a toy or the chance to run and romp.

If your dog is not doing as you say, either he didn't hear you (which is unlikely because dogs have pretty good hearing), he didn't understand the request (have you trained it properly?) or there are distractions (competing motivational factors are around).

Quick Tips:

Make your command/request super rewarding, especially in the early days. Write a list of all the things your dog likes. You can then use those things after he does what you request. For example, a ten second sit means he can go out the back door for a run around. Lying on his bed for five seconds gets him a belly rub. Next time you ask him to sit down he will be far more likely to oblige.

Why does my dog...

Scratch constantly?

The Situation:

Do you ever get the feeling that your dog has ants in his pants? A little grooming and itching are normal for any animal but if your dog is constantly scratching then this may signify other issues.

Why:

Dogs are very good at picking up parasites. Check your dog weekly for signs of fleas and ticks. If unsure, visit your vet.

Another reason a dog may scratch is called 'displacement'. This is when a dog is confused and he reverts to something that is easy and feels good, such as scratching. It's a little like us humans chewing our nails when we are nervous. If he scratches during training it maybe that your dog simply doesn't understand your request. 'Lower the bar' and try to make sure he is successful in each training task.

Quick Tips:

If your dog is free of fleas yet still scratches around his collar area, it may be that he is pulling on the lead and the collar is giving him some discomfort. If this is the case, try a comfortable body harness and teach him the technique of 'loose lead walking'.

Carry out your own home vet checks on a weekly basis. Run your hands over your dog's body and feel for any lumps, bumps or differences between the limbs. Make it a pleasant experience by giving your dog a treat during this task, which also builds a strong bond.

Why does my dog...

Have smelly breath?

The Situation:

Your dog bounds up to you with a waggy tail and a great big 'smile' but as you bend over to pet him, you catch the pungent whiff of 'Dog Breath'. Is this normal or is something more sinister going on??

Why:

Many dogs have a certain odour on their breath. If you notice any sudden change, it can be an indication of a health issue such as kidney disease or a minor issue such as a tooth or gum problem.

Is it a fishy odour? It maybe due to an issue with the other end of the dog... his anal glands! Yes, Rover may be paying particular attention to that area with his mouth. So once again, go and visit your friendly vet.

Quick Tips:

Cleaning your dog's teeth is an option. You can get beef flavoured toothpaste which makes the task a little easier. And if your dog is on a wet diet, bones and some chews can help to clean the teeth.

Remember bad breath can be a symptom of other things. If you notice a change in your dog's breath, then a trip to the vets can put your mind at rest.

Why does my dog...
Moult?

44

The Situation:

Does your furniture, flooring and clothes have an interesting new accessory? A fine coat of dog hair? This can be frustrating for house-proud pet owners – but is there anything you can do about it?

Why:

It is perfectly normal for most dogs to lose their coat in stages. Owners often report a dog moulting more frequently when the summer comes or when the central heating starts up during the winter! It is a dog preparing his new cooler coat!

Have you noticed that your dog appears to be shedding more when you take him to unfamiliar environments such as the vets, or when you pick him up from the kennels? This can be a sign of mild stress. Dogs shed some of their coat when they are anxious.

Quick Tips:

If your dog is shedding suddenly, ask yourself if there is anything that may be causing him undue stress? A change in your routine? Another animal in the house? You can then work at making him feel more content.

Regular grooming can help keep your house and carpet clean. Take your dog into the garden on a windy day and go through his coat with a good grooming brush. Regularly brushing your dog's coat keeps it looking great because apart from removing any dead hair, it stimulates his skin to produce vital oils. Also, did you know, grooming can be a fantastic way to bond with your dog?

Why does my dog...

Pant?

The Situation:

Have you got a 'heavy breather' at home? Maybe it's after a big walk, or when it's getting hot outside or even when someone comes to the door – dogs pant for all sorts of different reasons – let's find out why...

Why:

Dogs often pant because it is a hot day or after they have exercised. That is normal. However, panting can also be a sign of stress and anxiety in a dog. As a trainer, it is often one of the first indications I notice that a dog is not a hundred percent happy.

Quick Tips:

If a dog is panting and it's not particularly hot or he has not returned from some exercise, ask yourself if there could be something causing your dog to feel anxious. If you are teaching him a new exercise, give your dog a two-minute break and try the exercise again making it a little easier. Have a look around; is there another dog, a person or object that may be making your dog scared?

At home, has he got a safe place where he can retire? In a noisy and chaotic household, if there is no place to escape he will get anxious and pant. Panting often goes along with other stress signs such as pacing up and down and sometimes barking.

Why does my dog...
Run away from the lead?

The Situation:

Have you ever been the park, ready to go home, only to end up chasing your dog around in circles – much to the entertainment of passers-by?

Why:

The lead has many powerful associations. When you get it out at home, it evokes excitement and often chaos. When a dog running free at the park sees the lead, it causes avoidance! The reason a dog often avoids the lead (and the owner) at the park is because the lead generally indicates 'home time'! Dogs are great at reading patterns and forming associations. The thought process is likely to be...Lead...Lead clipped on collar... walked out of the park...end of fun. So, to a dog in the park, seeing the lead means the end of fun!

Quick Tips:

Build a good recall. Call your dog back, show him some tasty snacks (sliced hotdog, for example) and drop some pieces on the grass between your feet. As he is snuffling around and enjoying the food, clip his lead on. Pause for ten seconds and then unclip it and send him back for more romps. The idea is that he gets called back and has his lead attached at least ten times during off-lead exercise. It becomes so frequent that the lead stops becoming associated with leaving the park and going home.

Why does my dog...

Not like his collar?

The Situation:

You have bought a fabulous leather collar for your new puppy but he doesn't appreciate it like you do! He runs around scratching at it and then looks decidedly miserable when wearing it.

Why:

To a puppy who has never worn a collar before, it is a piece of equipment that is completely alien. He doesn't know that dogs have been wearing collars for generations. It not only feels unusual but it makes a new jingling sound!

Once he realises that he can't remove it, he can go into something called, 'learned helplessness'. This is where an animal gives up, appears to 'shut down' and does not offer any behaviour. He may lie down grumpily or move around slowly.

Quick Tips:

Putting a collar on a new puppy and hoping for the best can work for some puppies but it can be a gamble. Far better to slowly get your puppy used to it and make it a positive experience from the start. It is simple. During meal times for a week, pop the collar on and present his meal as you normally would. The second he finishes the meal take his collar off. After a week of doing this, just leave the collar on and he should barely notice.

By using this method, straight away the collar predicts good stuff and whilst he is eating he is getting used to wearing the collar. You can still use this technique if your dog or puppy dislikes his current collar.

Ensure the collar is correctly fitted. You should be able to get three fingers comfortably underneath it when it is fastened.

Why does my dog...

Drag his bottom on

the floor?

The Situation:

It may make the most entertaining Youtube video, but if your dog is dragging his bottom across the floor, there's probably something going on....but what??

Why:

Whilst it may look comical, it is likely that there is an issue with that part of your dog's body. A common cause for 'scooting' is painful anal glands. These glands are found in the anus and contain a particular fluid which coats the faeces when he defecates. It is a form of scent marking for an animal. If the glands are infected or not emptying with the faeces, it can be the cause of irritation. He is likely trying to ease that feeling by dragging his bottom along the floor.

Another factor can be parasites such as worms. Eggs are often laid around the rectum. These eggs resemble small grains of rice.

Quick Tips:

Visit your vet to check your dog's overall health. Ensure your dog is on a good diet. If your dog's stools are firm, the glands are more likely to empty as they should.

Also speak to your vet about regularly worming your dog to prevent parasites.

Why does my dog...

Not like his photograph

taken – yes really?

The Situation:

While you might love taking 'selfies' and posing for family photo-shoots, some dogs react badly when a camera or smartphone is thrust at them. If yours is one, then read on...

Why:

You call your dog's name; point a little box at him and then flash! He is temporarily blinded! The first association with this device is not always a great one.

Your dog also knows your every facial expression and he is an expert reader of your body language. He spends a great deal of time studying you! Suddenly, when you get your camera out...you appear erratic and you change. This alone can be enough to spook your dog.

Quick Tips:

You can easily make the camera the predictor of good things. Simply show your dog the camera and within three seconds toss him a treat. Do this frequently before even taking a snap. When you get the camera out and you see your dog wag his tail or look pleased, hold the camera as you normally would, say his name, take a shot and within three seconds toss a treat. Again repeat many times. Soon, camera = treats. The association is a good one and you get him looking at the lens for that perfect photo!

Try and appear your usual self whilst you are lining up the shot. If you act very differently, he may well run off!

If possible, turn off the flash! You'll often get a better photo without the flash, which can create a particular type of 'red eye' in the image.

Why does my dog...

Behave at home but not

in the park?

The Situation:

"Sorry...he never does that at home!" If you're constantly saying this to strangers at the park because your dog seems to forget his basic training, then you can start to wonder whether all those hours of schooling were just a waste of time!

Why:

We call it 'location training'. Dogs are very good at context. He might believe that 'down' means put belly on kitchen floor. When you request 'down' on grass...he may not understand. Location is a big part of the training and the association of the task.

Also, we could have trained a dog to be obedient in the kitchen or the garden but add the hundreds of distractions that the park brings and the attention and focus drop. The distractions can be: other dogs; other people; scents; squirrels;

games; joggers etc. Distractions are a big part of training and can hinder our progress. We need to train around distractions but they need to be added slowly!

Quick Tips:

Begin training in an area of low distractions, like the kitchen or garden. Your dog then has a basic grasp of what is expected and just how rewarding training can be. You can then start the same exercises at the park. Start the exercise from the beginning again. Don't train when the park is busy, but perhaps when there is one dog at a distance. The next time it could be two dogs or a few people around and so on. Go easy, each session should be successful - build on success and make it rewarding; slowly add distractions and train in a variety of locations.

Do expect your dog to behave slightly differently in novel environments, for example, when walking along a different route. Perhaps use a higher value treat than usual (chicken?) in new environments.

Why does my dog...

Frequently pass wind?

51

The Situation:

We love our dogs. We'd do anything for them. And we excuse them almost anything. But learning to live with a dog that constantly produces odours that could knockout a hippo can be a challenge too much for some owners! If you're finding your dog's natural emissions difficult to stomach, you might wonder if there's anything you can do - or is this just the price of living with your best (but rather smelly) pal?

Why:

There are many types of dog food on the market. Not all dog foods suit all dogs all the time! Your dog's food may not suit him and producing excess gas can be an indication of this. It could also be that he is exercising too soon after eating.

Quick Tips:

Consider changing to a quality dog food. When changing foods, slowly introduce the new brand by feeding three-quarters of the old food together with a quarter of the new food. And on the third day, half of the old food together with half of the new food. Over the course of ten days gradually switch until you are feeding all new food. It is a weaning process that allows your dog to adjust to his new diet without upsetting his stomach.

If your dog is gulping the food, it can also cause wind. If you have a gulper, consider one of the various interactive feeders available. These can slow down the eating process. And try not to encourage exercise too soon after he has eaten his meal.

Why does my dog...

Rip up his toys?

52

The Situation:

You've just returned from the pet shop with some fantastic toys for your dog. He is pleased with them - so pleased that half and hour later they are in pieces with stuffing everywhere!

Why:

Dogs are predators and still have a built-in behaviour of dissecting and gutting. This is often seen when a dog shakes a toy and spends time pulling out the stuffing. Fortunately, this behaviour is usually carried out on inanimate objects like toys. The removal of the stuffing and the dismembering are perhaps an imprint of a long past behaviour.

Quick Tips:

Keep the delicate toys special and out of the way, in a toy box or on a shelf, for example. Try and make the game itself more exciting so that your dog does not feel the need to make his own entertainment with the toy. Remove the toy when you have finished playing or when he starts chewing, ripping and mouthing it.

When playing with your dog, make the toy 'alive'. Hide it behind your back and bring it out, move it across the floor and let him follow it! A dead toy is often a boring toy or a toy to rip up!

For 'power-chewers', there are special toys available that are stronger and supposedly last longer.

Why does my dog...

Freeze when another dog

approaches?

53

The Situation:

Another dog comes bounding over to greet your dog with a waggy tail. It looks like a fun time will be had but your dog simply freezes still and does not move. Is this rude? What's with that?

Why:

When two dogs greet, they use their specific body language to indicate intention. Do they want to play or not? When anxious, dogs have three options...Fight, Flee or Freeze. By standing still and looking away, the dog is indicating that he is not a threat and he may play. Remaining impassive is a good policy, as the approaching dog will not feel threatened and it is more likely to become a friendly encounter.

Quick Tips:

If your dog is on a lead, remain calm and try and keep the lead slack. Any tension in the lead may cause further stress in your dog. Talk happily to your dog, 'Look, here comes a friendly dog'. You are then telling your dog there is no problem and your dog will know his owner feels good too.

Never allow your off-lead dog to approach a dog that is on a lead or training line. It doesn't help that dog, who is often on a lead for a reason. Help the dog and owner by calling your dog away and walking in the opposite direction.

Why does my dog...

Run around in circles?

The Situation:

Your dog starts interacting with another dog in the park and appears to run in circles around the other dog and around you. This can make training with a long line a little tricky as you get wrapped up in the ever-decreasing line.

Why:

Many breeds, such as the Border Collie, are hardwired to herd other animals. Think of a sheep dog. You may have a dog as a companion and not for working purposes, yet a little of the working behaviour is there ready to show itself if encouraged.

It is often like a switch that flicks on when the dog's excitement level reaches a certain point. Some dogs even add nipping to their circling repertoire.

Quick Tips:

Hardwired behaviour such as circling and often nipping usually appear when the dog is very excited. The pre-programmed actions almost spill out. If it is an issue, stop any training sessions and any play before the dog starts getting over-excited. Call your dog back to you and have two minutes chill time to allow your dog to cool down before restarting.

Ensure your dog has plenty of exercise and stimulation. Why not get your dog to chase a tennis ball and circle that instead? He is likely to circle anyway, so make it an appropriate game.

Why does my dog...

Wag his tail when he

sees me?

55

The Situation:

You arrive home with your shopping bags and he leaps at you wagging his tail frantically. His tail is so strong it feels like a pole hitting your legs. As he moves into the front room, the coffee table goes flying along with everything on it!

Why:

Dogs release pheromones from certain points on their bodies. This social odour gives information to other animals. You see this when two dogs greet, they usually sniff the other dog at those points (ears, muzzle, groin and anus). A nervous and unsociable dog will almost lock his tail under himself, denying the other dog a chance to find out about him. In contrast, a happy and social dog may wag his tail loosely to spread the pheromones around.

Although humans can't knowingly detect a dog's social odour, when your dog is greeting you it is believed his tail is wagging in an effort to circulate that information.

Quick Tips:

If his tail is a cause of destruction, simple training can save the day. Teach a polite sit when he greets people. A sit keeps him in one place and where his tail remains safe! Request a sit when you enter the house and only when he sits does he get your attention, your eye contact and perhaps a tasty treat. He will learn that sitting pays off!

Why does my dog...

Lick his lips?

56

The Situation:

When I take my dog to the vets, he never looks at the vet and I have noticed he licks his lips frequently. He also does this when he meets large dogs at the park. Why is that?

Why:

It is thought that if a dog licks his lips and there is no food present, it is a part of his body language and a form of communication. It is perhaps a signal of appeasement. It has been observed that if a dog is uncomfortable in his environment, he will 'lip lick'. Something around him may be considered a threat and is probably worrying him. In the two examples given, he may feel uncomfortable with large dogs and the vet.

Quick Tips:

If you notice your dog lip licking and there is no food nearby have a think as to what could be causing your dog to feel uncomfortable. It could be something as simple as being too close to another dog, in which case you can help by moving him away calmly. At the vets, if he is backed into a corner, step away and give him a little space. Obviously look at the context of the situation. Lip licking is a useful piece of body language which can help us to help our dogs.

Why does my dog...

Bow towards other dogs?

57

The Situation:

A small dog runs up to your dog at the park and after thirty seconds your dog is bowing before him. Is he stretching? Is he going to pounce? Also, whenever he drops a ball at your feet he assumes this position. Why does he do this?

Why:

When his front half is lower than his rear end, it is a strong piece of body language we call a 'playbow'. It is believed that dogs show this position as an invitation to play, possibly because a dog cannot appear threatening to another dog if his head is so low it is touching the floor! It is great to watch two dogs playing especially when you see two dogs playbowing at the same time.

Quick Tips:

You can teach a playbow so that when you say 'Bow' your dog assumes that position, a little like when you request a sit. It's a neat trick and it can be very useful when introducing your dog to other dogs. If your dog has been asked to do a playbow, he will appear unthreatening to the other dog, meaning they are more likely to get along and even play.

Why does my dog...

Stalk?

The Situation:

Has your dog turned into the canine equivalent of an SAS agent? He spots his target (a dog, cat, or even a random object) and before you know it he's creeping up, trailing, following, and shadowing like a crack commando unit, before giving chase.

Why:

Stalking is part of a dog's hardwired predatory sequence of 'see...STALK...chase...grab...bite...kill...eat.' Fortunately, the last parts of the chain have been bred out of most dogs. But the first three pieces remain and have been encouraged in breeds such as the Greyhound racing (see/chase) and the Border Collie herding sheep (stalk). Predatory behaviour is typically very quiet, it has to be or their evening meal would scatter and run! The stalking is a very efficient way to get as close to the prey as possible whilst reserving their energy ready for the chase.

Domestic dogs often trip into this behaviour and may stalk their tennis ball or even other dogs. However, with domestic dogs, the stalking of other dogs is likely to be a method to get as close as possible to play.

Quick Tips:

If the stalking results in nothing but a game then appreciate how it came to be and don't let it concern you.

If your dog stalks cats and small animals, a simple way to interrupt the behaviour is to use your dog's name and within seconds produce his favorite toy. Toss it in the other direction to the critter. You are then using the same drive but replacing the target for something more appropriate. It also gives the animal being stalked a chance to escape and leave. Try and interrupt the sequence before your dog starts stalking, just after he has spotted the target.

Why does my dog...

Show his belly?

The Situation:

You're used to your dog being on all four paws, or lying down, but some dogs seem to like to see the world from a different angle, lying back and showing their belly. Legs in the air like they just don't care!

Why:

The dog's ancestor, the wolf, often uses this display. A nervous wolf may show his stomach as a way of appeasing the situation. He is likely saying that he is no threat to the other wolf. It is a piece of body language that our dogs retain. Many puppies display this behaviour, which is sometimes followed by urination. Dogs can work out that lying on their backs and showing their stomachs works quite well with us humans. They get a belly rub and everyone smiles. With other dogs, it can also get them out of trouble because the other dog is unlikely to show any aggression towards a dog who is appearing so passive.

Quick Tips:

If it is a problem and your dog gets his coat dirty on the floor when greeting people you can encourage a sit for a greeting instead. Before the dog rolls on his back request a sit and then he gets the greeting, the fuss and possible a tasty treat. If he then rolls on his back, the greeting stops, so it gets boring for him. He will learn that a sit produces the fun and showing his belly results in nothing special.

If the puppy is also urinating, you need to keep the greetings low key. Say hello and a quick fuss but end the greeting before it gets wet! And you can start teaching a sit for a greeting, as above.

Why does my dog...

Enjoy chocolate yet it's

bad for his health?

60

The Situation:

You come home to find coloured foil strewn all over the place and yet no sign of the chocolates. Your dog is snoring happily in the corner. Why do dogs love chocolate and is it safe?

Why:

Dogs like chocolate for the same reasons we do. Although we joke that dogs have 'cast iron stomachs', chocolate contains an ingredient called Theobromine, which is toxic for dogs. The darker the chocolate, the more Theobromine it contains. Too much chocolate can make a dog very ill and can kill.

Quick Tips:

If you think your dog has consumed any chocolate, no matter how small, call your vet immediately. If possible keep the wrapper and have an idea of the amount consumed. This information can help the vet regarding the Theobromine quantity and the next steps.

Keep all chocolate out of your dog's reach. Special attention should be paid at Easter and Christmas when there tends to be more chocolate around the house. Inform the whole family of the dangers of chocolate.

If you notice your dog pick up a piece of chocolate, try not to chase him. He will likely run off and eat it. Try and calmly call him to you and request a 'drop'. It is a good idea to develop a 'drop' or a 'leave' command before you really need to use it in an emergency situation. A quality dog training class can teach this in a positive way (no shouting, rattle cans or water sprays). Good training can save lives.

Why does my dog...

Give eye contact?

61

The Situation:

We'd like to think that when our dogs stare straight into our eyes, they're communicating their undying devotion and love. However, eye contact can have many meanings; so let's look at exactly what they are saying with their eyes.

Why:

In the canine world, direct eye contact between dogs can be a threat. If a strange dog looks directly at you and his body is very rigid, it could be a signal that he is not happy with you being near him. Growling or barking may often follow eye contact.

However, in a normal context we actively seek a dog's eye contact. It means he is focusing on us and will be more receptive. If you ask a dog who is looking at you to sit, you will have more chance of him sitting than if you are talking to the side of his head. You may have trained eye contact without thinking by simply giving him something he likes when he looks at you (his dinner for example).

Quick Tips:

You can train eye contact by only delivering what the dog wants as he looks at you. This can be his dinner, a toy, a chance to play with another dog or access to the garden. For example, have your hand on the door handle and the second he looks at your face, say 'good boy' and open it. This way he will give you eye contact whenever he wants something, as if he is asking, 'please?' Dog training improves 100% after teaching this form of attention and focus.

Why does my dog...
Walk more slowly on
the way home?

62

The Situation:

Your dog may have practically dragged you out of the front door at the start of your walk, and spent a good hour haring around, but when it comes time to go home, you may find he suddenly turns into a 'tortoise' and seems to go at a snail's pace.

Why:

It could be simply that your dog is tired but there maybe another reason! Whenever a dog pulls, look at what he is pulling towards. What is motivating that pulling, it's usually something he likes a lot. Similarly, if a dog is plodding and unmotivated, ask yourself why.

If he is scared and reluctant to walk towards something like a dustcart, then respect that and workout why and perhaps avoid it. The excitement of the park could be so great that he doesn't want to go home. He's been having lots of fun and maybe already eaten one of his main meals. There is nothing great about going home now!

Quick Tips:

Don't feed your dog before his walk or park visit. This keeps him hungry and motivated. Grab a handful of his dry food and take it out with you. When he does something you really like, give him a piece of the kibble. He will start to repeat the good behaviour more readily in the future.

Once you return home allow about half an hour for him to cool down and feed him the rest of his meal. Suddenly going home will become more worthwhile because he gets to finish his dinner!!

Why does my dog...
Raise his paw?

63

The Situation:

"Aw, that's so cute." This is the normal reaction when dogs raise their paws. We can't help interpreting it as a sign of affection. But what is he really trying to communicate with this simple gesture?

Why:

It is a piece of body language, which we can view as 'uncertainty'. But with all body language you must view it in context. Is your dog perhaps unsure of something ahead during a walk? Has he spotted a cat, a bird? It is almost a moment frozen in time...should he move forward or should he remain still?

It may also be a learned behaviour. If you have smiled and given him attention during this paw lift, it's rewarding and he may repeat the action many times in the future. Or has someone been teaching him a 'beg' or 'paw'?

Quick Tips:

If he has been taught 'paw' or 'beg', a problem can occur when your dog wants something. He will beg and raise a paw because that is what paid out for him during the training. If you have bare shins, it can get quite painful regularly having claws scratching whilst you eat your toast, for example.

If it is a problem, stop teaching a 'paw' or 'beg' command and teach a good 'sit' or a 'down' in a similar manner to how you taught the 'paw'. If your dog is asking "please", which would you prefer? Sitting static in one place or a paw regularly scratching your shin? Maybe stop rewarding the paw lift and reward an alternative behaviour like a sit instead?

Why does my dog...

Bare his teeth?

64

The Situation:

Dogs have a great range of facial expressions, but when they start baring their teeth, and look more like Dracula than Scooby Doo, it can be worrying for owners.

Why:

Dogs arrive with hundreds of signals to indicate their particular mood. Whilst other dogs are usually able to decipher each subtle signal, humans usually struggle. Dogs rarely bite! In nature biting and fighting is 'expensive behaviour' and fraught with risk. Animals would rather posture than exert energy and risk a damaging fight.

Before a bite, the signals are often in this order... stiffen/growl/show teeth/air snap/bite. So a dog showing his teeth is usually an indication he is not happy! A domestic dog should have no need to display any of these signals if he is social, confident and comfortable in his environment. Have a think why your dog is so anxious that he feels the need to display this warning signal of baring teeth.

Quick Tips:

Never ignore what a dog who bares his teeth is trying to tell you, just as you should never ignore growling behaviour. They are both vital pieces of information. If you continue or reprimand, next time the dog may skip those signals and go straight to the bite. You end up with a dog that bites with zero warning! Instead, walk away and consider why your dog feels anxious. Is he too close to a perceived threat, does he feel the need to guard items or areas, are there other dogs nearby making him worried? Maybe he's anticipating a reprimand from you? Walk away and consider what to do next time so the situation will not re-occur.

Why does my dog...

Sleep all day?

The Situation:

It's midday; you glance lovingly at your dog and he is completely out of it and in dreamland. You finish reading the paper and he is still asleep. For large periods of the day, he's about as animated as the armchair in the corner. Is he ok?

Why:

If the health of a dog is good, it is quite normal for him to frequently sleep. Puppies are growing and developing and older dogs need sleep to restore and refresh. On average, an adult dog, over two years old, requires about fourteen hours of sleep per day! Puppies and elderly dogs require even more!

It can depend on the size, age, breed and the amount of exercise and stimulation the dog receives, but dogs sleep often.

Dogs are naturally 'Crepuscular', which means they are more active around dawn and dusk, which are often the times you will see your puppy zooming around the house looking for exercise.

Quick Tips:

If you notice your dog suddenly sleeping more than usual or not sleeping as much as before, speak to your vet to ensure there are no underlying health issues.

Because dogs are Crepuscular, the best times for a fun walk or a game would be first thing in the morning, before their meal and just before their evening meal Expect lots of snoring at stages during the day and follow the old adage of 'let sleeping dogs lie!'

Why does my dog...

Guard his food?

The Situation:

You've lovingly prepared your dog's dinner, and he's so thrilled to see you when you give it to him. But once he's started eating, you may find he starts freezing and growling as you walk past him. This is classic food guarding behaviour.

Why:

We must remember that dogs are animals and food is a valuable resource. It is very natural to want to protect it from other animals, including the two-legged kind!

The growling is a warning and a sign that the dog is not confident about you being around. Does he think you will steal it? We have to teach our dogs that we are not a threat and that there is plenty of food that we supply.

Quick Tips:

We can help puppies realise we are not a threat by calmly walking past as they eat and dropping pieces of yummy chicken by their food bowl as they eat their usual food. If you do this for a few weeks, your puppy will actually feel great when you are nearby during meal times. Your presence predicts good things...not a threat. 'When my owner is near and I am eating, tasty chicken pieces fall near my bowl!'

You can make a situation worse by removing the food bowl whilst they eat. This tells the puppy or dog that you are annoying and a possible threat to their eating. Better to slowly add the food into their food bowl...be a giver not a taker!

Listen to a growl, respect it and realise your dog is not happy. Do not get into a confrontation, which will make the situation worse. Seek help and work it through so your dog has nothing to fear during his mealtime.

Why does my dog...

Guard his toys?

The Situation:

You've treated your pet to a lovely new toy, which he quickly takes and starts to play with. But get too close and you may find your dog growling or barking to ward you off. He's guarding his toys and keeping them to himself.

Why:

If a toy is special to your dog it becomes a high-value resource, similar to food. Guarding high-value resources in nature is very normal behaviour. Growling and posturing is a clear sign that the dog does not want to give up what he considers valuable. If your dog is growling when you approach his favorite toy, it may indicate he is not at all confident around people. We have to ensure that dogs do not feel the need to growl and feel anxious.

Quick Tips:

From day one, teach your dog how to play appropriately with toys. Produce the toy, play and then exchange it for a similar one to encourage interaction. He will learn that giving up a toy means he usually gets another one!

Keep a favorite toy either on the shelf or in a drawer. You can use it as a reward when training or for short games with your dog.

Why does my dog...
Toilet in the house?

68

The Situation:

You can't believe it! You've created a lovely home for your dog, but he seems to be intent on going to the toilet inside rather than out. This frustrating behaviour can cause real problems for owners if not handled properly.

Why:

If your dog is healthy, he may have never learned to pee and poop in the garden. He may even have been inadvertently rewarded for messing in your house. Any form of attention, even yelling, can be seen as rewarding. Once the indoor habit is established it can take some time to break the cycle. And although we cannot smell it and have cleaned it, the scent of pee and poop can remain, triggering a repeat performance!

Quick Tips:

It's up to owners to make the peeing and pooping outdoors more rewarding than indoors. And for that, you must be with your dog when he gets it correct! For puppies, be in the garden with them every hour. Ignore your puppy until he has done a pee or poop and then gently praise and then present a piece of yummy chicken or low-fat cheese. For an adult dog, pop out in the garden with him every two hours and follow the same method. Fortunately, this procedure should not have to be carried out late at night/early morning.

Snacks and praise occur if he pees or poops in the garden, meaning he will learn to hold on longer. Over time, your garden trips will be less frequent. "Be there when he gets it right so you can let him know and reward him!"

If your dog messes in the house...nothing great happens. Do not reprimand but calmly remove him to another room and clean up the mess with a cleaning solution designed for the purpose.

Why does my dog...

Scrape his back feet on

the grass?

The Situation:

Your dog has just done his 'business' and because you are a good dog owner, you are in the process of picking it up. He decides to scrape his back feet on the grass you are standing near, sending tufts of grass and earth flying towards you. What's that about?

Why:

It is believed that when a dog keeps his back legs stiff and scuffs his back feet over the grass, he is adding more scent to the area. Animals are very scent driven and dogs will leave urine and faeces as their unique scent message to other dogs. Dogs have scent glands between the pads on their feet, so they are perhaps wiping this scent on the grass. The disturbance of the ground is also a sign that, 'Rover was here!'

The scraping of the feet is also often accompanied by a ridged body and snorting. So aside from the scent reasons, this can also be considered posturing to inform other dogs that he is in the area.

Quick Tips:

Some dogs can get caught up in a pattern of increasing foot scraping. If it is something you don't want, you can stop it fairly easily. Just before your dog starts the scraping, pleasantly say his name, show him a treat and slowly toss it into the grass. He will focus on hunting for the treat rather than posturing and scraping.

Why does my dog...

Rush out the door

before me?

The Situation:

Everyone's keen to leave the house for a pleasant walk, but some dogs are intent on rushing through the front door before you. In fact, not just the front door! Many pets, want to go ahead of their owners through any door.

Why:

It is nothing to do with your dog wanting to be 'pack leader' but dogs often go through doors before us because they can! They are faster and often want to know what excitement is ahead of them. Outside the house, for example, is one big playground!

Whilst we may consider it rude behaviour, to a dog it is very natural and he is not misbehaving, especially if he has not been taught to wait. There are also many times you may want your dog going through a door before you...into a rainy garden for the 10pm pee, for example? However, it can be dangerous if your dog dashes out of the front door and into the street. Some simple doggy manners are required.

Quick Tips:

Teach your dog to sit at the threshold and to 'stay'. Once you are through you can call him to join you. If you find this training tricky, you can pop your dog's lead on and have someone hold your dog back as you say 'stay' and step through.

Another method is to request a sit at the threshold and toss a small treat back into the room as you step through the door. Your dog will learn to wait to anticipate something nice appearing behind him...not through the door ahead.

Why does my dog...

Chase squirrels?

71

The Situation:

An enjoyable walk in the park can be quickly interrupted when your dog suddenly rockets across the grass and clumsily attempts to climb trees in order to chase squirrels!

Why:

Dogs are predators and some breeds have more of a 'prey drive' than others. Also to a dog, a small and furry twitching creature is going to attract his curiosity - especially if it runs off, which is often what squirrels do. You may find the Terrier breed more fixated with small furry animals because they are hardwired to dispatch them. Dogs that have been used to work with the gun, such as Spaniels, will also have more of a need to chase critters. The same applies Greyhounds and other sight-hounds.

Quick Tips:

The good news about squirrels is that they disappear quickly up a tree so your dog should still be in sight! Although it can be done with lots of diligent training, it can be extremely difficult to call away a dog in full chase mode. Don't wait for the chase.

There will be several seconds after your dog sees the squirrel and before he chases. His body language may change. Learn to spot this change and interrupt the flow. Dogs 'see' and 'chase'. Using a whistle as a recall can distract your dog into navigating towards you for a treat. Say his name or clap your hands and as he looks around at you, produce a treat or his favourite toy for a game of...chase. Meanwhile, the squirrel disappears.

Why does my dog...

Chase rabbits?

72

The Situation:

Your normally well-behaved dog can seem impossible to manage if he gets fixated on chasing a rabbit. A peaceful country walk might turn into a scene from a comedy show as you chase your dog, who's much more interested in chasing down Bugs Bunny!

Why:

Some breeds have a higher prey drive than others. Prey drive is what makes a Greyhound race; it is what makes a Jack Russell kill twenty rats in one minute and a Cocker Spaniel flush game from bracken. It is very natural for a dog to want to chase small furry things especially if they run which then provokes that chasing prey drive. Many dogs come pre-programmed to want to do this and for some the 'wiring' is very strong. And the more it is rehearsed, the more the need to chase rabbits.

Quick Tips:

If your dog enjoys a good chase, you can redirect him towards something you may consider more appropriate. There are toys available, which are critter-like toys on the end of a cord connected to a pole. By whipping the pole around, you can make the toy come alive and become rabbit-like. If your dog plays regularly with this 'flirt pole', he will exercise that need to chase and may be less likely to chase when out walking.

Your best chance to stop a dog chasing is to gain his attention the split second after he has spotted the rabbit. Once he is off it is very difficult to call him back. Just after he has spotted the rabbit call his name or pip your whistle and interrupt him. Call him towards you where he can get a treat or even better, the chance to chase a 'flirt pole' (toy on a cord). You redirect his chase!

Why does my dog...

Kill rodents?

73

The Situation:

Your pet is a loving, friendly companion and you adore all their quirks...apart from the fact that he seems to turn into a psychotic killing machine whenever a rodent is nearby. Some dogs will proudly display their hunting skills in front of you – but for other owners – the only evidence they have is being brought the corpses of victims! Nice!

Why:

Some breeds of dog have a high prey drive. Humans have encouraged this drive in order to use it in a practical way. For example, when villages were over-run with rats, Terriers would be brought in. A Terrier can kill many, many rodents in quick speed. Even though your cuddly dog may never have been employed to kill rats and mice, it is in his general make-up. He may be 'hardwired' for this behaviour.

Quick Tips:

It is very difficult to deny a dog, particularly a Terrier, the opportunity to carry out a behaviour he is bred for. So prevention is the best option. Keep small furry pets away from your chasing dog.

Allow your dog to practice this behaviour in an appropriate and controlled way with a good game. Purchase a rodent-like toy and tie some string to it. You can now make it come alive!! A few short, three-minute games a day will allow your dog to exercise this behaviour and you may find he is less interested in chasing real rodents.

Why does my dog...

Scratch the floor?

74

The Situation:

Whether it's your new laminate flooring or a lovely fresh rug, some dogs seem to think your home décor would be improved by them scratching ferociously at it!

Why:

Digging is a 'fixed motor pattern' for a dog. This means they are almost born with the action although they don't quite realise that it works better when digging is carried out in soft earth. In the wild, a dog is likely to dig a small pit to sleep in. This pit would conserve heat in the winter and keep him cool in the summer.

So very often a dog may scratch the floor before lying down. Dogs are also very good at noticing a reaction, if your dog scratches in a mock digging behaviour and it gains rewarding attention it is very likely to be repeated.

And remember, even a reprimand is attention which can be seen as rewarding. So the digging action starts off as a 'fixed motor pattern' and can become a learned behaviour.

Quick Tips:

Give your dog a really comfy bed with a couple of blankets. He can then dig at his bedding without damaging your carpet or wooden floor.

If he does scratch at something inappropriate, then use his name in a pleasant way to interrupt and guide him to his bedding area where he can happily carry on.

Why does my dog...

Not eat when I'm out?

75

The Situation:

Sometimes you just have to go out when it's normally your pet's dinnertime. So the simple solution is to leave your dog his dinner, where he can easily access it. But often normally ravenous hounds decide to go on hunger strike when you're not there, leaving their bowls full and their tummies empty.

Why:

Dogs are social creatures and like to be around other creatures, especially during mealtimes. Have you noticed your dog chew a bone or a toy when you are eating? Therefore, a dog will feel more comfortable eating when you are around. Also, a dog who gets anxious when you are away from him will certainly not be thinking about his belly. Anxiety shuts down the digestive system, so if your dog is not eating when you are out, consider why. Does he bark and is he destructive when you are out? If so work around a plan to tackle 'Separation Anxiety'.

Quick Tips:

Try upping the tastiness of the food you are leaving him with. Many people leave a Kong stuffed with a mixture of yummy snacks mixed with the dog's usual meal. This helps a dog cope when alone and makes it a slightly more pleasant event.

Initially give an interactive toy like a stuffed Kong when all is calm. A good time is in the evening when the household is watching television together. If you repeat this for a few nights, the Kong has a good association. Now you can use it before you leave the house and he can chew and eat and feel slightly better when you are not there.

Why does my dog...

Get on the chair the

minute I've got off it?

The Situation:

If you let your dog sit on the sofa or other furniture, you may find a strange game of 'musical chairs' happening. You've hardly stood up and before you know it, your pet has jumped into your place and is now sitting very comfortably!

Why:

It's a warm spot, it's comfortable and it's clearly a good place because you were sitting there. Dogs do not lie on our seats to dominate or to be a pack leader. It's simply a good place to be and to be off the floor means your dog can see all around and get an idea of what's occurring in the house. It's a safe, snug place.

Quick Tips:

If it is something you don't want, prevention is the best option. Have a set-up for when you leave the house. Guide your dog to the kitchen or his bed and give him a tasty pre-filled Kong before you walk out of the house. This gives him something to do rather than stressing out and looking for comfy seats!

And although it is cute to see your dog curled up on your vacated seat, if you laugh smile or pet your dog when he's there, you are saying it's ok. You are rewarding him and the behaviour may be repeated.

If it's not something you consider a problem, place a blanket on the seat...this gives your dog a clear signal and it keeps your seat free of dog-hair! He is allowed on the furniture only when the blanket is present. If he leaps up without the blanket being seen, guide him off as passively as you can.

Why does my dog...

Stick his head out of a

car window?

77

The Situation:

You're cruising down the road, and even though you've provided your pet with a lovely blanket, and a safety harness, he seems intent to stick his head out of the window - ears flapping in the wind.

Why:

For an animal that gains most of its information via the nose...scenting whilst on the move must be like watching a movie in fast forward! He must be in paradise! He is gaining tons of information about the area. He will be learning about the whole environment at super fast speed and likely trying to establish information about the dogs in that area.

Quick Tips:

Although it can be fun for your dog, and look cute, it can also be dangerous especially if your vehicle is travelling at speed. Insects and other debris can smack into his eyes and face. If it's something your dog enjoys, you can open a window slightly, so his nose doesn't quite stick out. He can still air-scent but it's safer.

Alternatively, give him something else to do on car journeys. Put some of his dinner in a Kong chew toy. If it's dry food, moisten it and squash it in. He will spend the journey time licking and chewing instead.

Why does my dog...

Chase his tail?

The Situation:

You provide your dog with toys, and give him long walks, and you've been to dog school. Yet he seems to spend his time running in circles chasing his own tail!

Why:

This can be a coping mechanism for a stressed dog. When a dog is anxious and needs to shake off stress, tail chasing can be an easy and reliable option. Once the endorphins start flowing it can be an addictive habit.

Also, we often laugh and point because it looks cute. This strengthens the behaviour and makes it more likely to be repeated in the future. Your dog now has a full blown habit.

Quick Tips:

Ensure your dog has adequate stimulation during his usual day. Stimulation can include sniffing, meeting other dogs, going to new environments and playing games. Games like fetch and tuggy are perhaps a better way for him to 'shake off' any stress.

If your dog starts tail chasing, just walk out of the room without looking or saying anything. If he doesn't stop in ten seconds call him to you and pick up a toy and have a quick thirty-second game. You are then redirecting his behaviour onto something more appropriate. Also consider why he is doing it. Is it stress related? Is his day-to-day life fulfilling enough?

Why does my dog...

Yawn?

The Situation:

Your dog is meeting your friend for the first time; he hasn't been out all day. Your dog looks away and lets out a five second yawn! Much laughter ensues. Is your friend boring? Is Rover dog-tired?

Why:

A yawn can be considered a stress sign. If your dog is not tired and is in a potentially stressful environment, you will notice the odd yawn. It can be one of a number of visual stress indications, which we can read. Others can be: ears flat, tail down and looking away.

Not all stress is bad however. Excitement carries an amount of stress. Look at the whole situation and help your dog if you believe the environment is causing him undue anxiety and stress.

Quick Tips:

If it is an unfamiliar person approaching your dog when your dog yawns, stop the introduction. Always allow a dog to approach the unfamiliar person and allow him to do it in his own time. Once he is close enough, the stranger can deliver a tasty treat. Your dog soon learns to trust the stranger and starts to feel good in their presence.

If you spot your dog yawning and it's possibly a stressful environment (noise, people, other dogs) give him the opportunity to move away and allow him time to get used to the new environment, people, dogs or objects.

Why does my dog...

Smile?

The Situation:

You know he's an animal – but you're certain that when your dog looks into your eyes and grins, that he's actually smiling at you.

Why:

Some dogs appear to be smiling and it can generally mean a good thing. If a dog is relaxed and content, the muscles around the lips are loose which gives the impression of a smile. It's likely that dogs do not intend to smile as we do, but it is a great indication that the 'smiling dog' is a happy and relaxed dog.

If a dog is baring his teeth...this is not a 'happy' smile and is most likely a warning to back off.

Quick Tips:

If a dog's mouth has a tight appearance, it can mean that the dog is stressed. Look at the situation and environment and figure out why. A stressed dog is a dog more likely to react and possibly bite.

Never approach an unfamiliar dog and be aware that a tight, stiff looking body and a closed mouth usually indicates an anxious dog. Anxious dogs can bite! Even if the dog is 'smiling', always allow the dog to approach you!

Why does my dog...

Steal the television

remote and chew it up?

81

The Situation:

Ok, who's got the remote? Is it between the sofa cushions? Nope! It's in your dog's bed and looking worse for wear! That's the third remote control to act as a chew toy! Why does he always target the remote control?

Why:

Dogs are very scent focused and your remote control contains the whole family's scent. At some point, each member of your family has held it. The unit is made of a rubbery material, which is porous (it contains microscopic pores). This means it holds scent pretty well! Your remote is a familiar item, which reminds your dog of you!

Also, the TV remote almost resembles a dog toy. It contains different colours and it's rubbery! Puppies, in particular, have a need to chew and the remote may have been all that he could find at the time.

Quick Tips:

Keep the remote control off the sofa, off the coffee table and out of reach from your dog, on a shelf perhaps. Give it a safe home! Once your family know where the remote lives, you'll also save time searching for it under the sofa cushions!

Ensure your dog has chew toys. Put a tiny smear of peanut butter in a Kong. Rub your hands over the Kong to give it a familiar odour, which he recognises, and leave your dog with that.

Why does my dog...

Bark at the vacuum

cleaner?

The Situation:

You've put it off, now is the time to clean the house. The instant you wheel out the vacuum cleaner from the cupboard, your dog is barking at it and charging towards it like it should run out of the house, never to return. Turn the vacuum cleaner on and it's even worse. Cleaning the house is never fun but this really is a chore!

Why:

Modern vacuum cleaners contain many bright coloured parts, which almost resemble your dog's toys! Add the fact that it moves, it blows air out, it's noisy and interacts with humans and you have something that is completely confusing for your dog. For many dogs, it's an object to approach and avoid, almost at the same time.

Quick Tips:

From the day you get your puppy, you can help him realise the vacuum cleaner is not an excitable game or a scary monster. With it switched off, calmly bring it out into the room and quietly allow your puppy to investigate it. Perhaps place some of your puppy's dry food near it and on it. He can eat some of his dinner this way. Leave the cleaner there for a few days without turning it on. A few days later turn it on for five seconds whilst hand feeding your puppy. This prepares him for the noise.

When you decide to vacuum the house, have a tasty Kong prepared. The second you turn on the vacuum cleaner, show him the Kong and place it in his bed or crate. Allow him to enjoy the Kong as you clean. He'll soon look forward to you cleaning as he gets a yummy Kong to chew on! You can apply this method for an adult dog also!

Why does my dog...

Circle before lying down?

The Situation:

You send your dog to his bed and it's twenty seconds before he lies down! He is turning and turning. It looks like an elaborate ritual and he must be getting dizzy surely?!

Why:

It is believed that it is an old fixed behaviour carried through from the days when wild dogs slept in the outdoors. Circling is thought to make a space in long grass, move away any creepy crawlies and perhaps warm up the spot he will sleep in.

You may have also noticed your dog often sleeps with his tail covering his nose. Again, this is thought to be an old action carried through generations, which was designed to keep his nose warm in the cold.

Quick Tips:

You may find that if your family and friends have witnessed this circling and laughed, the circling has increased. The turning ritual has now been rewarded and strengthened. Therefore, what was once an instinctual act is now also a learned behaviour.

It's certainly not an action that can be harmful but if you wanted your dog to settle quicker, you could teach a 'down'. This 'down' can soon be changed into a 'settle', which is a more relaxed looking 'down'.

Why does my dog...

Have a wet nose?

The Situation:

As your dog greets you, he is 'nose first'! Wet nose prints all over your trousers! Why is his nose wet? Has he got a cold?

Why:

A wet nose is often the sign of a healthy dog! And if a dog is dehydrated his nose will be bone dry. A wet nose is also a good nose for scenting and scent is used a heck of a lot by dogs! Dog's noses are usually coated by a thin layer of mucus, which helps absorb various scent particles.

Did you know every dog has a unique nose-print?! Take a closer look at your dogs nose and you will see tiny patterns.

Quick Tips:

Don't worry, your dog can be quite healthy and have the occasional dry nose but a cold wet nose is a good nose!

Carry out regular visual checks of your dog's nose. Grass seeds can get stuck in the passages and start growing. A sign of blockages can be frequent sneezing. Consult a vet if unsure.

You can put his nose to work by attending Nosework Classes where your dog is taught to locate various hidden items using his primary sense! Nosework can often tire a dog out more than physical exercise and it's something your dog will really enjoy.

Why does my dog...

Nip at my feet and ankles?

85

The Situation:

Do you end up doing a version of 'River Dance' while your loving dog seems intent at nipping your toes or ankles? This may be entertaining for your family to watch, but is this behaviour normal?

Why:

Breeds like the Border Collie are hardwired to round up sheep. You may have a domesticated pet dog but this behaviour is deeply ingrained throughout generations. Sheepdogs occasionally nip the sheep they are herding. So your 'out of work' sheepdog may occasionally nip human feet. The behaviour sometimes shows itself when the dog is over-excited. It is like the hardwired behaviour turns on and starts spilling over.

Quick Tips:

This is very difficult to stop because it is an ingrained action. It would be like preventing a dog from sniffing a hedge! Instead of preventing it, be aware of triggers. It usually occurs when a dog is over-excited.

When he gets over-excited and before he starts nipping, give him his favourite toy. This redirects the behaviour. Should he nip your ankles and feet, request a sit, Teach a good sit when he is not nipping. You can then request it when you really need to. He can't be nipping and sitting at the same time.

Never laugh and dance around because you are then rewarding the behaviour...if you do, expect more nipping in future!

Why does my dog...

Bark at people wearing

high viz jackets?

86

The Situation:

Your super-social dog wags his tail as soon as any person looks at him. But why is it he freezes and barks at anyone supposedly in authority and wearing a high visibility jacket?

Why:

This issue often starts when your dog was a puppy. In many cases, people wearing high viz jackets create noise and movement. Think bin-men and various manual workers. Your puppy likely came into contact with these people and could have been spooked by all the noise the 'scary' men were making. The memory was not men, it was not boots...it was high viz jackets. This association is then carried through, meaning your dog is now anxious around anyone in that particular type of jacket. Barking is frequently a mechanism to move the scary thing away and to create distance. To your dog, high viz jackets are spooky and scary!

Quick Tips:

If you know of somewhere where there are people wearing this particular type of jacket, you can set up a series of trials. Have some yummy treats on you (chicken or cheese). Keep a fair distance from the person in the high viz jacket and as soon as your dog sees the person...feed! Have that person go out of view or gently remove your dog to behind a tree, for example, and stop feeding. Whenever your dog sees a high viz jacketed person, the food appears. The jacket soon becomes the predictor of snacks and not fear!

Why does my dog...

Bark at people wearing

uniforms?

The Situation:

You have a friendly dog – he loves people...that is, unless they are wearing some kind of uniform! There's something about a person in uniform that can make dogs go crazy.

Why:

To your dog, people in uniform often act slightly differently to familiar people. They are often acting assertively and directly. Consider a Police Officer; he may walk quicker than most people or even be seen running. So your dog sees someone acting slightly differently, perhaps in a stressful situation and the person looks different with a hat or helmet. If your dog isn't sure, rather than run away, he may stand and bark. Barking is intended to make the 'scary thing move away'. When you consider a postman does exactly that, his barking is actually rewarded.

uick Tips:

er drag your dog towards anything he is wary of. Give your dog space between the person and him and make out it's no big deal. Tell him, 'Hey it's only a policeman', for example. You can also help by giving him a tasty treat as soon as he sees the uniformed person. Your dog can learn that people in uniform aren't that scary...good stuff happens when he sees them!

Why does my dog...

Ignore me when I call?

The Situation:

A peaceful walk changes when your dog spots another who has just entered the park. You can shout as loud as you like. Nope... he runs and doesn't look back.

Why:

What would make an animal, such as a dog focus on us? Why would a dog look at us when there is another dog around? Because he 'should'? Because he 'respects us'? Not really. Because he will get told off? That would be a further reason not to come back! As owners we have to appear as valuable and almost as exciting as the distraction of the other dog! If a dog associates his owner with something fantastic, he is far more likely to respond.

Quick Tips:

If it is a regular occurrence, don't allow your dog to rehearse this unwanted action of running off. Use a training long-line to prevent your dog from bolting off.

On walks, at the park, in the garden, randomly say your dogs name and follow it within two seconds with a piece of yummy chicken. After a while, your dog will almost have a reflex to his name because his name means chicken!!

When you need to use his name in the park, he will be more likely to focus on you.

Bring some of your dog's breakfast to the park with you. When he looks up at you for any reason, he gets a few pieces. This encourages him to 'check in with you' and focus.

If you think your dog is about to run off, you need to use his name pretty quickly to interrupt the pattern. The more he goes into full chase, the less chance you have of getting his attention. The second he spots the distraction/attraction say his name and follow it with a treat, which you can toss gently away from the distraction.

Why does my dog...

Chase bike riders?

The Situation:

You are having a pleasant lead walk around the block when very silently a person cycles by. Immediately your dog pulls hard to the end of the lead and drags you a few metres in an attempt to chase the bike. Is he trying to race it?

Why:

Many dogs have a chase instinct. It is almost a reflex. Anything moving faster than your dog can trip this chase instinct. Most dogs will simply chase and if they catch the bike they do nothing. The chase is better than the catch for many dogs!

Quick Tips:

If you face this issue, you can set up a training situation. Have someone cycle past. The second your dog sees the cycle, say your dog's name for attention, turn 180 degrees on the spot with your dog and walk in the opposite direction. Produce a yummy treat for your dog just after you turn. This kills the chase instinct and soon your dog learns it is not worth running.

Alternatively, stand near a road where cyclists go past. And move as far away from the road as you can. Relax with your dog. As soon as your dog sees a cyclist, pop a treat into your dog's mouth. When the cyclist has gone out of sight, the treats stop arriving. Soon a cyclist can mean treats from you and not a chance to chase!

Why does my dog...

Get hiccups?

90

The Situation:

What's that noise? Is it on the television? No it's your puppy hiccupping! It looks a little distressing, it can't be comfortable. Is he ok?

Why:

Although it can sound quite alarming at times, this is very common with young developing puppies. It is quite normal and may be a result of the dog eating too quickly or gulping lots of air whilst eating. Stress and anxiety can also be contributing factors.

Puppies often grow out of hiccupping.

Quick Tips:

You can purchase interactive food dispensers, which makes the dog work for the food. Therefore, he will not 'wolf it down'. Balls with a hole in allow his dry meal to fall out slowly when rolled. He quickly learns that rolling the ball around the floor results in food.

For long necked dogs such as Lurchers and Greyhounds, you can raise their food bowl, which may help with digestion and so prevent hiccups. It can also help with their overall posture.

If you have an older dog that suffers from hiccups, why not spread his meals out across the day. Feed three or four smaller meals rather than two large meals.

Why does my dog...

Get bored of playing?

The Situation:

Dogs should want to play, right? You pick his toy off the floor ready for a fun game, he comes over looking excited but within 30 seconds he's off finding his own fun.

Why:

Dogs are attracted to novel items. A toy that has been lying on the floor for a while soon becomes stale and boring. And the toy needs to be part of you, so you have to act excited and appear fun to your dog. A game with your dog is a great way to build that bond and a game can make a fantastic reward for a recall, for example.

Dogs, particularly puppies, also have very short attention spans.

Quick Tips:

Aside from the odd chew toy, keep your dog's toys off the floor and out of reach. By bringing out a different toy every day, it makes that toy appear fresh, new and exciting.

Always end the game when your dog still wants to play and before he gets bored. Ideally keep the games under three minutes and play frequently. So play frequently but in quick regular sessions!

You can incorporate play in training. Request a sit, count to two and then praise and whip out a toy for a game. Now, request a sit and count to four...praise and play a game. You are building a stable sit (duration) as well as teaching self-control! Have fun!

Why does my dog...

Bark at dogs on the

television?

92

The Situation:

You're watching your favorite TV presenter as he is stroking a sad looking rescue dog. Your dog leaps up from his slumber, runs towards the flat-screen and barks and barks. Does he really think there is another dog in your living room?

Why:

With the advent of high definition televisions and life-like quality, is it any wonder a dog can see images on our television? Years ago when we had a huge box in the corner of the room it contained technology, which produced images that were perhaps harder for a dog to see. But these days, it's there, in our living room, in full High Definition glory! Aside from the image, the sounds can also be enough to alert some dogs into barking.

Quick Tips:

So is it visual or auditory? Turn down the volume and see if your dog still barks. If he doesn't, it may be the sounds of other dogs that cause him to feel alarmed.

If your dog does bark at the flat screen television, don't make a big issue of it...if you shout at your dog, it may sound to him like you are barking too! Ignore the barking; perhaps get up and walk away. You are then not making it any worse and he realises that barking ends your attention.

Ideally, if you are about to settle down to watch Pet Rescue, for example, have a tasty chew available for him. As soon as he spots the dog on television, he gets the chew on his mat. Soon, dogs on television equal good things.

Why does my dog...
Run along the fence
barking?

The Situation:

You let your dog out at the end of the night for a wee and all he does is run alongside the neighbour's fence and bark...and bark and bark! This is not great for the community spirit!

Why:

If there was something super exciting over the fence at one time, your dog will remember. It may have been another dog, some screaming children or a cat. Your dog at the time probably tried barking to communicate but it was a one-sided conversation so frustration builds and builds. It can be particularly bad if a dog the other side of the fence joins in. The frustration built up can appear to be aggressive.

Quick Tips:

If your dog has just started barking, try and interrupt it before it gets too intense. Walk him out on a lead if necessary so he can do his business. You can build a really good whistle recall so just before he starts this barking, you whistle him in for a treat or even his dinner!

Ensure your dog has plenty of exercise and stimulation every day. Playing, sniffing, and running are all things that help to enrich your dog's day. A bored dog is more likely to bark at the universe!

Why does my dog...

Bury toys and bones?

94

The Situation:

Your flowerbed will never look the same again now you have a dog. Buried under mounds of fresh earth are not seeds but his bones and toys. Why does he do it?

Why:

If a dog has a prize item, he may feel the need to put it somewhere safe. Underground is fairly safe! It is thought to be a behaviour carried over from their wild ancestors; the need to bury tasty food out of sight from other animals so that they can return later to finish it. Your dog is using the flowerbed as a larder or a toy box.

Quick Tips:

Give your dog his own little patch of ground where he can dig and hide articles. Regardless of what you try he will likely bury items anyway, so give him his very own patch. If you find items buried elsewhere, replant them in his own patch to encourage him to look there.

If your dog does value his toys to that extent, leave a couple laying around for him and don't remove them. Perhaps put them on his bed or in his crate. If he feels his toys are safe he will perhaps have less need to hide them in the earth.

Why does my dog...

Not go out in the rain?

The Situation:

It's bedtime, you are tired and a little cold and it's pouring with rain outside. Usual routine, open the back door so your dog can relieve himself before bed and he sits there looking up you! You step outside and try and encourage him but he's not budging and you're getting wet! Is he scared of rain?

Why:

Breeds with a thin coat such as the Staffordshire Bull Terrier can certainly feel uncomfortable in the rain, just as we might without an umbrella. However, some dogs may have learned that they'd rather stay in the warm, thank you very much! These are the smart dogs! It can be learned behaviour. Dogs can learn that when it's raining the family usher lots of 'ahhhhhhs' and plenty of attention when they stay in one place, out of the rain.

Interestingly, recent research suggests that noise-phobic dogs are reluctant to venture out into the wet because the moisture amplifies sound. The reason could, therefore, also be due to a fear of loud noises.

Quick Tips:

In the early days, dash outside with your dog, shut the door and simply wait, use an umbrella if necessary. Give him ten minutes. If he is looking like he wants to go back inside, wait it out until he does a pee and then praise him and allow him back in. He can soon learn that when he pees you open the door and it gets him out of the rain sooner, so in future he may actually pee quicker when it's raining.

Why does my dog...

Drool in the car?

96

The Situation:

Driving along looking in your rear-view mirror and your dog is dribbling! On arrival, you let him out of the car and there is a small pool of saliva in the back of the car.

Why:

It is very likely that the car makes your dog feel unwell. Drooling often precedes vomiting. It can be the association of a bad car journey. Many journeys in the dog's life are traumatic, from the first car journey away from his mother and siblings to a trip to the vets for an injection. Your dog may think the car equals scary things! That's enough to make anyone sick. He may also have had a sickness episode in the car making the journey unpleasant and so it becomes a cycle.

Motion sickness can also be a factor just as it can be for us humans.

Quick Tips:

Whilst medication is available from your vets you can still work on making car journeys' the predicator of good things, not bad things. Work on it daily over a few weeks. Day one, pop him in the car, sit in the driver's seat, shut the door, pause and then let him out again. Maybe he goes indoors to have his dinner? Day two, repeat day one but start the engine for thirty seconds. Turn it off and let him out for his dinner indoors. Day three, put the engine on for one minute and end the rehearsal. Day four, repeat the previous days exercises but drive along the road for one minute and return home. Build slowly over two weeks until you are driving him somewhere pleasant like the local park for a fun walk. You need to keep the journeys short, so he doesn't have time to feel nauseous and the destination should be pleasant, like fun at the park or dinner at home.

You can also experiment with putting him in a different place inside the car where motion sickness may not be such a factor. Also, a new location in the car will have no previous bad associations for him.

Why does my dog...

Look guilty?

97

The Situation:

You put your key in the door, step in and there is your dog greeting you but he appears guilty. His ears are down and he is avoiding eye contact. Sure enough, he's had an accident in the kitchen and he knows it. He knows he's been naughty, doesn't he?

Why:

It is unlikely that a dog understands the (human) concept of guilt. Dogs live for the moment, have a different understanding of time and often forget actions that have taken place a short while ago.

Studies have shown that what we see as 'that guilty look' is actually the dog responding to our body language. We appear concerned with whatever naughty act he may have done and perhaps look different and upset! This is especially true if he has been reprimanded in the past. His body language (ears down, avoiding eye contact, low tail) is thought to be appeasement. He is trying to calm the situation of seeing an upset person. He is reacting to you and not any previous 'mistakes' or damage.

Quick Tips:

If you walk in and find your dog has been naughty (in your eyes), there is little point in reprimanding him. All he sees is you pointing and looking angry. Try and remain passive and clean up any mistakes out of sight from your dog. Work on the issue before it occurs, so it doesn't happen again.

Why does my dog...

Steal food off the kitchen counter?

98

The Situation:

You've just finished making the children's sandwiches ready for school and the doorbell goes. The second your back is turned your dog has cleverly put two paws on the counter and has a sandwich in his jaws! Within seconds, it's gone as he runs off! Does this happen often?

Why:

Dog's are natural scavengers and this is the type of behaviour which has made them the successful species that they are today. Their nose is so much more powerful than our own, allowing them to detect food and where it is. If only one opportunistic leap and grab pays off, there is a very good chance it will occur again!

Quick Tips:

Prevention is better than cure. Never leave food on the counter where it is accessible. Invest in a bread bin where any food you are preparing can be put should you be quickly called away.

Ensure your dog has lots of stimulation and activity. Training classes can help with this. A bored dog will find his own entertainment and jumping up at the counter can be entertaining ...and rewarding!
Do not reprimand, as dogs can pick up the wrong association and have a negative emotional response to anything else in the area, including you! He won't know what he is being punished for.

Most dogs grow out of this counter-surfing if ALL attempts are made to be unsuccessful attempts.

Why does my dog...

Mount all dogs?

99

The Situation:

You are standing at the park putting the world to rights with the other dog owners when you notice your dog is mounting one of their dogs. Cue lots of embarrassed laughter. Park walks may be avoided in the future?

Why:

For puppies and young dogs it can be simply a case of practicing the mechanics of mating. Mating is a natural urge and all species are pre-programmed to do it. This explains why your young male has just mounted your neighbour's male labrador. Practice. The behaviour is enhanced when the dog is playing and the play gets intense. Play is thought to be practice for most adult behaviour (which also includes hunting). Over-excited play sometimes tips over into the action of mounting and to your dog, although he's not sure why, it feels good.

He may, of course, be an adult dog with adult equipment! If a female dog is 'in season', it is very hard to stop the natural act!

Quick Tips:

If you have an adolescent at about eight months of age and he mounts cushions, people's legs and other dogs, you have two choices:

A) Keep him from getting over-excited during play and quickly interrupt any mounting behaviour. Call him back to you in the park and allow him to cool down for a minute.

B) Consider neutering. Speak to your vet about this.

It must be said that neutering does not always stop this if the act has been practiced enough times that it has become a habit. Prevention and good training can help.

Why does my dog...

Zoom around the house?

The Situation:

Every day your puppy runs so frantically around the house he is almost running vertically along the walls. It's chaos. Cups go flying! Why does he resemble a 'wall of death' daredevil bike rider?

Why:

Dogs are Crepuscular, which means they are most active around twilight. Dusk is often when this crazy behaviour is seen. It is normal behaviour and thought to be a young dog blowing out a little bit of tension whilst getting a quick burst of exercise. It can also sometimes be seen when you enter the house after leaving your dog. It can be his way of dealing with the excitement and the pleasure of you returning home. It is common and most young dogs grow out of it.

Quick Tips:

If you have cups and ornaments nearby, simply open the back door and allow him to zoom around in the garden. 'Zoomies go outside'? Be very passive when he is charging around. Any attention, even reprimands, may be seen as rewarding, which then makes this crazy behaviour even more fun than it already is!

Ensure he is on a good quality diet. Food is thought to affect heightened activity.

Why does my dog...

Like this book?

101

The Situation:

Whenever you pick up this book, your dog gazes up at you affectionately. And as you read, as if by magic, he sits without you even asking! How does a book do that?

Why:

I'm hoping you have gained some knowledge from this little book. You may have smiled as you read it. The methods used to address the 100 dilemmas are positive, fun and will not harm your dog. You are now a happier owner and your dog is full of joy!

Quick Tips:

Keep this book handy at all times. Dogs are animals and can sometimes learn new and unwanted behaviours. This book is always here to help with those!

If your dog has been ever-so-slightly mischievous and is safe, you are safe and no damage has been caused...smile! A dog without mischief is a dull dog! We like a little mischief! Enjoy your dog, he should make you smile every day!

About The Author

Tony Cruse

Expert positive dog trainer, Tony Cruse, has a wealth of experience helping owners understand their dog, improve their pet's behaviour and enjoy a successful relationship with their canine companion.

He has instructed at several successful training schools, and worked at a busy rescue kennels. He owns and runs Tc Dog Training in Chelmsford, Essex, providing group training, one to one consultations and specialist workshops.

Recommended by many veterinary surgeries, Tony is a member of the Association of Pet Dog Trainers (APDT UK) and The Institute of Modern Dog Trainers (IMDT), both of which have a strict code of practice. He abides by the kind and fair principles of training, which are built on the science of canine behaviour.

A sought-after speaker, writer and trainer, Tony has appeared on many radio stations (including BBC Radio 2), and writes regularly for Your Dog Magazine, Britain's best-selling canine publication.

To discover more about Tony's work, please visit www.tcdogtraining.co.uk

"Tony will help you 'get into your dog's mind' and see things from your dog's point of view."

Dr. Ian Dunbar
Founder of the Association of Professional Dog Trainers

Index   Page

Printed in Great Britain
by Amazon.co.uk, Ltd.,
Marston Gate.